CW00595090

THE
MERLIN ENGINE SPITFIRES

HANDBOOK

First published by Air Ministry 1940-44 & 1949-51

This combined edition
First published by Crécy Publishing 2021

ISBN 9781910809716

Printed in Bulgaria by Multiprint

published by

Crécy Publishing Limited
1a Ringway Trading Estate, Shadowmoss Road, Manchester M22 5LH
www.crecy.co.uk

CONTENTS

Merlin
66, 67, 70, 71, 76, 77 & 85
Aero-Engines
Air Publications 1590 P, S & U
Volume I

Merlin
Operating Instructions
Section 1

The Spitfire I Aeroplane
Merlin II or III Engine

Spitfire F.IX Aeroplane
Merlin 61 Engine

Spitfire 16

A·P·
1590
P·S & U
VOLUME I

Merlin

66 67 70 71 76 77 & 85

AERO — ENGINES

Prepared by direction of the
Minister of Aircraft Production

Promulgated by order of the Air Council

AIR MINISTRY

Reprinted by Authority:
McLAREN & CO. PTY. LTD., MELBOURNE

AMENDMENT RECORD SHEET

Incorporation of an Amendment List in this publication should be recorded by inserting the Amendment List number, signing the appropriate column, and inserting the date of making the amendments.

A.L. No.	Amendments made by	Date
1 5	Incorporated in this reprint	October, 1944

This leaf issued with A.L. No. 7
July, 1944

AIR PUBLICATION 1590P, S and U
Volume I

NOTE TO READERS

Air Ministry Orders and Vol. II, Part 1 leaflets either in this A.P or in the A.P.'s listed below, or even in some others, may affect the subject matter of this publication. Where possible Amendment Lists are issued to bring this volume into line, but it is not always practicable to do so, for example when a modification has not been embodied in all the stores in service.

When an Order or leaflet is found to contradict any portion of this publication, the Order or leaflet is to be taken as the overriding authority.

When this volume is amended by the insertion of new leaves in an existing section or chapter, the new or amended technical information is indicated by a vertical line in the outer margin.   This line is merely to denote a change and is not to be taken as a mark of emphasis.   When a section or chapter is re-issued in completely revised form, the vertical line is not used.

Each leaf is marked in the top left-hand corner with the number of the A.L. with which it was issued.

LIST OF ASSOCIATED PUBLICATIONS

The following is a list of Air Publications and Air Diagrams which are related to this publication.

Title							Air Publication Number
Technical Notes for Rolls-Royce Engines	...	...	...	...	...	...	2308
Rotol external cylinder variable-pitch propellers		...	...	...	...	...	1538E
Electrical equipment	...	...	...	...	...	...	...	1095
Aircraft Hydraulic equipment	...	..	...	...	...	...	...	1803
Stromberg Carburation equipment	...	...	...	...	...	...	2239C
Aero-Engine Ignition equipment ...	...	...	...	...	...	...	1374

Also the relevant aircraft and Pilot's Notes Air Publications.

Title					Air Diagram Number
Stromberg Injection Carburettor (Merlin Aero-Engines)	...	...	..	...	2310
Stromberg Injection Carburettor—Theoretical diagram	...	...	...	...	2656
Aero-Engine Exhaust Flame Characteristics	...	...	...	...	...	2490

LAYOUT TREE FOR A.P. 1590 P, S and U

MERLIN 66, 67, 70, 71, 76, 77, and 85

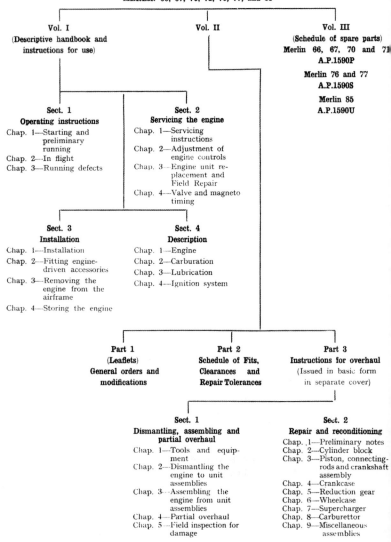

Vol. I
(Descriptive handbook and instructions for use)

Vol. II

Vol. III
(Schedule of spare parts)
Merlin 66, 67, 70 and 71
A.P.1590P

Merlin 76 and 77
A.P.1590S

Merlin 85
A.P.1590U

Sect. 1
Operating instructions
Chap. 1—Starting and preliminary running
Chap. 2—In flight
Chap. 3—Running defects

Sect. 2
Servicing the engine
Chap. 1—Servicing instructions
Chap. 2—Adjustment of engine controls
Chap. 3—Engine unit replacement and Field Repair
Chap. 4—Valve and magneto timing

Sect. 3
Installation
Chap. 1—Installation
Chap. 2—Fitting engine-driven accessories
Chap. 3—Removing the engine from the airframe
Chap. 4—Storing the engine

Sect. 4
Description
Chap. 1—Engine
Chap. 2—Carburation
Chap. 3—Lubrication
Chap. 4—Ignition system

Part 1
(Leaflets)
General orders and modifications

Part 2
Schedule of Fits, Clearances and Repair Tolerances

Part 3
Instructions for overhaul
(Issued in basic form in separate cover)

Sect. 1
Dismantling, assembling and partial overhaul
Chap. 1—Tools and equipment
Chap. 2—Dismantling the engine to unit assemblies
Chap. 3—Assembling the engine from unit assemblies
Chap. 4—Partial overhaul
Chap. 5—Field inspection for damage

Sect. 2
Repair and reconditioning
Chap. 1—Preliminary notes
Chap. 2—Cylinder block
Chap. 3—Piston, connecting-rods and crankshaft assembly
Chap. 4—Crankcase
Chap. 5—Reduction gear
Chap. 6—Wheelcase
Chap. 7—Supercharger
Chap. 8—Carburettor
Chap. 9—Miscellaneous assemblies

This leaf issued with A.L. No. 7
July, 1944

AIR PUBLICATION 1590 P, S and U
Volume I

MERLIN 66, 67, 70, 71, 76, 77 and 85

AERO-ENGINES

LIST OF SECTIONS

Note.—A list of chapters appears at the beginning of each section

FRONTISPIECE.—MERLIN TWO-SPEED, TWO-STAGE AERO-ENGINE FITTED WITH STROMBERG CARBURETTOR

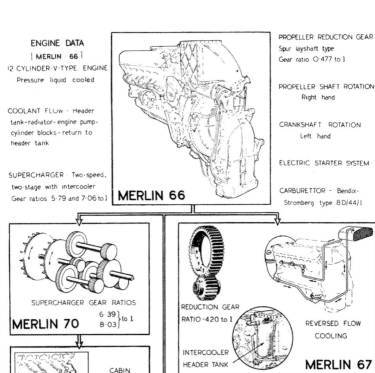

ENGINE DATA
[MERLIN 66]
12 CYLINDER·V·TYPE ENGINE
Pressure liquid cooled

COOLANT FLOW - Header
tank-radiator-engine pump-
cylinder blocks-return to
header tank

SUPERCHARGER · Two-speed,
two-stage with intercooler
Gear ratios 5·79 and 7·06 to 1

MERLIN 66

PROPELLER REDUCTION GEAR
Spur layshaft type
Gear ratio 0·477 to 1

PROPELLER SHAFT ROTATION
Right hand

CRANKSHAFT ROTATION
Left hand

ELECTRIC STARTER SYSTEM

CARBURETTOR - Bendix-
Stromberg type 8D/44/1

SUPERCHARGER GEAR RATIOS
6·39
8·03 } to 1
MERLIN 70

CABIN
SUPERCHARGER
DRIVE
MERLIN 71

REDUCTION
GEAR
RATIO
420 to 1
GEARBOX DRIVE
MERLIN 85

REDUCTION GEAR
RATIO ·420 to 1

INTERCOOLER
HEADER TANK

REVERSED FLOW
COOLING
MERLIN 67

SUPERCHARGER
GEAR RATIOS
6·39
8·03 } to 1
MERLIN 76

CABIN SUPERCHARGER
DRIVE
MERLIN 77

ENGINE IDENTIFICATION CHART

This leaf issued with A.L. No. 7
July, 1944

INTRODUCTION

1. The Merlin aero-engines covered by this Air Publication are of similar design to the Merlin 61 series. Merlin 85 engines have the accessories grouped together, mounted on a separate gearbox behind the aircraft bulkhead and driven from the engine accessory drive on the rear port side. The engines are designed to operate on 100 octane fuel and to maintain their maximum power at high altitudes.

2. Each cylinder block mounted on an inclined upper facing of the crankcase comprises a light-alloy skirt and detachable head between which the upper flanges of the separate steel liners are sandwiched. The liners, therefore, float at their lower ends in the crankcase, the block being held in compression by the main securing studs. Each cylinder has four valves—two inlet and two sodium-cooled exhaust valves. All valves of each cylinder block are operated from a single centrally-disposed overhead camshaft through a system of individual tappet fingers.

3. The balanced six-throw crankshaft is supported within the crankcase in seven lead-bronze lined main bearings. The connecting-rods are H-section steel forgings and are of the forked type on the left-hand or "B" side, and of the plain type on the right-hand or "A" side. A divided steel block is bolted to the forked rod and retains a flanged thin steel shell lined with lead-bronze in its bore which works directly on the crankpin. Similar split bearing shells are also fitted to the plain rod working on the outer surface of the forked rod block. In each case locating lips are formed on one half of each shell to engage with slots in the cap.

4. Bolted to the front of the crankcase is the reduction gear casing, and mounted at the rear of the crankcase is the wheelcase, which houses the components transmitting the drive from the rear end of the crankcase to the accessories. When a cabin supercharger is fitted, the crankcase and reduction gear casings have similar extensions on the starboard side to those provided for the combustion starter drive fitted on Merlin 32 engines. In place of the combustion starter, however, a cabin supercharger is fitted to maintain normal atmospheric pressure in the aircraft cabin. On the port side of the crankcase a small centrifugal pump is driven which circulates coolant for the supercharger intercooler cooling system. The wheelcase houses the upper and lower vertical drive units, the magnetos, the main coolant pump, the idler gear which drives the oil pumps and the hydraulic pump, the fuel pumps and the electric generator drive. A hand and electric turning gear is also housed within the wheelcase.

5. The two-speed two-stage supercharger unit is attached to the rear of the wheelcase. It is of the tandem two-rotor centrifugal type, driven from the rear end of the crankshaft through three centrifugally-loaded clutch wheels which absorb the high inertia loading resulting from rapid acceleration and deceleration, torsional fluctuations being absorbed by a spring-drive shaft. The drive to the supercharger is transmitted through only one of the centrifugally-loaded clutch wheels in the case of the low gear, and the remaining two transmit the drive in the case of the high gear. The control of the clutch wheels, which determines whether the low or high gear ratios are in action, is effected by means of a system of forked levers which are actuated by an intermediate camshaft. The camshaft itself is actuated by a servo piston operated by scavenge oil pressure and controlled by a piston-type valve having a two-position lever. This may either be coupled to a hand-control in the cockpit or to an electro-pneumatic unit operated by a two-position switch in the cockpit, by means of which the low or high gear ratio may be selected. In the latter case the supercharger is automatically controlled with respect to altitude. A liquid-cooled intercooler unit of the flattened tube type is placed between the supercharger delivery and the main central induction manifold for the purpose of lowering the temperature of the mixture delivered to the cylinders. The header tank may be formed integrally with the intercooler assembly or, alternatively, be a separate tank.

6. Carburation is provided by a twin-intake, Stromberg injection type carburettor forming a complete assembly secured to the supercharger intake. The correct quantity of fuel is determined by the weight of air flowing through the intakes and is then positively injected and diffused in the supercharger intake eye. The carburettor operates in conjunction with a pneumatically actuated variable datum boost control unit.

7. The lubrication system of the engine is of the dry sump type, one pressure pump and two scavenge pumps being employed. These three pumps form a unit which is attached to the rear end of the lower half of the crankcase. Besides the principal function of lubricating the engine, the lubricating system also supplies main pressure oil for actuating the constant-speed propeller, and scavenge oil for actuating the two-speed supercharger servo control cylinder. A proportion of the main pressure oil is transformed by a reducing relief valve to low pressure for the purpose of lubricating the reduction gear, camshafts, rockers and auxiliary drives.

This leaf issued with A.L. No. 7
July, 1944

OPERATING LIMITATIONS

for

Merlin 66, 67, 70, 71, 76, 77 and 85

Aero-Engines

OPERATING LIMITATIONS

Merlin 66, 67, 70, 71, 76, 77 and 85 Aero-Engines

CONDITIONS OF FLIGHT	BOOST lb. per sq. in.	R.P.M.	OIL TEMP. °C. (Inlet)	COOLANT TEMP. °C. (Outlet)	TIME LIMIT
TAKE-OFF	+12 Merlin 66, 67, 70, 71, 76, 77 ——— +18 Merlin 85	3,000 max. ——— 2,200 min.	15° min.	60° min.	5 minutes or 1,000 ft.
CLIMB SPECIAL EMERGENCY (1 engine stopped)	+12	2,850	90°	125°	1 hour
COMBAT	+18	3,000	105°	135°	5 minutes
MAXIMUM CRUISING	+7	2,650 ——— Merlin 85, High (F.S)gear, 2,850	90°	105° *115° Emergency	
DIVING (Throttle lever at least one-third open)	+18	3,150	---	---	20 seconds

* Short period emergency on fighter aircraft and for special application only

FUEL CONSUMPTION FIGURES AT MAXIMUM CRUISING CONDITIONS†

Engine type	Low gear	High gear
Merlin 66, 67 and 85	80 gall./hr	80 gall./hr.
Merlin 70, 71, 76 and 77	80 gall./hr.	83 gall./hr.

† These figures are ground test figures. Flight test figures will be issued later by amendment action.

LEADING PARTICULARS

(MERLIN 66, 67, 70, 71, 76, 77, and 85)

(1) General

Type of engine	Supercharged, geared, pressure liquid cooled V-engine, fitted with a two-speed, two-stage, liquid-cooled supercharger with intercooler
Number of cylinders	12
Arrangement of cylinders	Two banks of six cylinders each with an inclined angle of 60°
Bore	5·4 in.
Stroke	6·0 in.
Swept volume	1,648 cu. in.
Compression ratio	6·0 to 1
Supercharger—	
Type	Two-stage, two-speed
Gear ratios (Merlin 66, 67 and 85) ..	5·79 to 1 and 7·06 to 1
Gear ratios (Merlin 70, 71, 76 and 77)	6·39 to 1 and 8·03 to 1
Propeller reduction gear—	
Type	Spur layshaft, single reduction
Ratio (Merlin 66, 70 and 71) ...	0·477 to 1
Ratio (Merlin 67, 76, 77, and 85)	0·420 to 1
Direction of rotation—	
Propeller shaft	Right-hand
Crankshaft	Left-hand
Cylinder numbering	Propeller 1A, 2A, 3A, 4A, 5A, 6A ⎫ 1B, 2B, 3B, 4B, 5B, 6B ⎬
Weight of engine, nett dry	1,650 lb. + 2½ per cent. tolerance

(2) Performance

	Low gear	High gear
Merlin 66, 67, and 85		
International power rating	1,400 b.h.p. at 9,250 ft.	1,310 b.h.p. at 19,000 ft.
Combat power rating	1,705 b.h.p. at 5,750 ft.	1,580 b.h.p. at 16,000 ft.
Merlin 70, 71, 76 and 77		
International power rating ...	1,375 b.h.p. at 13,500 ft.	1,255 b.h.p. at 25,250 ft.
Combat power rating	1,655 b.h.p. at 10,000 ft.	1,475 b.h.p. at 22,250 ft.

(3) Oil

Type	Specification D.T.D.472B with or without Additive No. 1 (see Vol. II leaflet, A.P.1464/C.37—W)
Consumption at maximum cruising conditions	6 to 20 pints per hour
Pressures—	
Main	
Normal	45 to 80 lb. per sq. in.
Minimum in flight	30 lb. per sq. in.

(4) Ignition

Firing order	1A, 6B, 4A, 3B, 2A, 5B, 6A, 1B, 3A, 4B, 5A, 2B
Magnetos—	
Number	Two
Type	B.T.H. C6SE–12S or Rotax NSE12–4 (Stamped "A" indicating for use at high altitude)
Direction of rotation (looking in drive end)	Port, clockwise; Starboard, anti-clockwise
Speed of rotation	1·5 engine speed
Contact breaker gap	0·012 in. ± 0·001 in

Timing—
    Fully advanced ...   .   Port 50° before T.D.C.
                                              Starboard 45° before T.D.C.
    Fully retarded   ...   .   Port, 30° before T.D.C.
                                                Starboard 25° before T.D.C.
    Sparking plug types   ...   .   K.L.G.: RC5/2
    Sparking plug gaps   ...   .   0·012 in.

(5) **Carburation**
    Carburettor ...   .   Stromberg type 8D/44/1 double entry
    Fuel ...   .   100 octane (Stores Ref. 34A/75)
    Maximum fuel demand   ...   ...   153 gallons per hour
    Pump pressure to carburettor   ...   15 lb. per sq. in.

(6) **Valves**
    Valve timing (with 0·020 in. tappet
      clearance—all valves)—
      Inlet opens   ...   .   31° before T.D.C.
      Inlet closes   ...   .   52° after B.D.C.
      Exhaust opens   ...   .   72° before B.D.C.
      Exhaust closes   ...   .   12° after T.D.C.
    Running clearance ...   . $\begin{cases} 0·010 + 0·002 \text{ in. (inlet)} \\ 0·020 \pm 0·002 \text{ in. (exhaus} \end{cases}$

(7) **Coolant**
    Engine coolant—
      Type   ...   .   Pressure liquid (70 per cent water + 30 per cent
                   ethylene-glycol to Specification D.T.D.344A)
    System—
      Merlin 66, 70 and 71   ...   ...   Normal flow
      Merlin 67, 76 and 77   ...   ...   Reversed flow
    Coolant for intercooler system—
      Type   ...   .   Pressure liquid (70 per cent. water + 30 per cent.
                   ethylene-glycol to Specification D.T.D.344A)

(8) **Starting system**
    Type   ...   .   Hand and electric turning gear

(9) **Propeller**
    Type   ...   .   Rotol, 4-blade external cylinder 35° pitch range
                   with constant-speed control

(10) **Accessories**
    The following accessories can be fitted to these aero-engines. Those used in any particular
installation are specified in the appropriate aircraft Air Publication.

Accessories	Speed ratio relative to crankshaft	Direction of rotation looking on driving spindle of accessories
Constant-speed governor unit	0·828	Clockwise
Vacuum pump	0·828	Clockwise
Electric generator	1·953	Anti-clockwise
Starter motor	91·56	Clockwise
Air compressor (camshaft)	0·5	Clockwise
Hydraulic pump (camshaft)	1·0	Clockwise
Engine-speed indicator drive (camshaft)	0·25	Clockwise
Hydraulic pump (crankcase)		
Horizontal drive	0·502 or 0·992	Clockwise
Vertical drive	0·81	Clockwise
Cabin supercharger (Merlin 71 and 77 only) ...	0·913	Anti-clockwise
Intercooler coolant pump	1·497	Anti-clockwise

OPERATING INSTRUCTIONS

SECTION 1

OPERATING INSTRUCTIONS

LIST OF CHAPTERS

Chapter 1. Starting and preliminary running

Chapter 2. In flight

Chapter 3. Running defects

Note.—A list of contents appears at the beginning of each chapter.

CHAPTER 1

STARTING AND PRELIMINARY RUNNING

LIST OF CONTENTS

LIST OF ILLUSTRATIONS

PREPARING THE ENGINE FOR SERVICE

1. The instructions detailed in the following paragraphs must be observed if the engine has been newly installed or has been standing idle for an appreciable period.

Installation

2. Check that all mounting nuts are completely tightened and locked safely.

Propeller

3. Check that the propeller is tight on the shaft and is securely locked in position.

Controls

4. Examine all engine controls, check for freedom of operation and lubricate where necessary.

Radiator flap

5. Check the opening and closing of the flap by means of the test button. The flap should open when the button is pressed and close when the button is released.

> *Note.*—It is necessary to ensure that an air pressure of 150 lb. per sq. in. is available before carrying out this check

Oil priming

6. Prime the engine with diluted oil as follows:—

    (i) Remove the pressure gauge connection fitted on the starboard side of the crankcase.

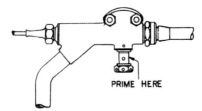

PRIME HERE

FIG. 1.—PRESSURE GAUGE CONNECTION ON MERLIN 71 AND 77

    (ii) Secure a suitable pump, such as the compressed air operated primer (Stores Ref. 4G/2342) described in A.P.1464B, Vol. I, Part 8, Sect. 9, to the connection as shown in fig. 2.

CONNECT HOSE BANJO OF OIL PRIMER

REMOVE PRESSURE GAUGE OIL CONNECTION

FIG. 2. PRIMING THE ENGINE OIL SYSTEM

    (iii) Remove the oil filters; this will enable surplus oil to drain and thereby obviate the possibility of flooding the engine.

    (iv) Prime the system with two gallons of approved oil diluted with 10 per cent. of aviation fuel, and at the same time rotate the crankshaft by turning the propeller, thus ensuring that the oil is fed to the bearings.

       Note.—Ascertain that the magneto switches are in the OFF position before turning the propeller.

    (v) Remove the priming connection, replace the pressure gauge connection and lock securely.

    (vi) Replace the oil filters.

    (vii) After the engine has been run up, inspect and clean the oil filters and also check that the normal air space exists in the oil tanks.

REAR FILTER

FIG. 3.—REMOVAL OF OIL FILTERS

Cooling system

7. The following points should be observed when filling the system.

    (i) The approximate quantity required to fill the system is:—

       $12\frac{1}{4}$ gallons, Spitfire aircraft.

    (ii) All coolant must be of the correct specification (*see* Leading Particulars) and should pass through a fine mesh gauze filter before entering the system.

    (iii) Open the vent cocks; these are situated on the pipelines between the radiators and thermostats in the case of Spitfire aircraft, in which a radiator is fitted in each wing.

    (iv) Remove the filler cap from the header tank and commence filling the system with coolant.

    (v) When a steady flow of coolant issues from the vent cocks, close them and lock securely.

       Note.—It should be observed that coolant is generally expelled before the air is released, and consequently the cocks should not be closed the moment that coolant issues.

    (vi) Continue filling the system until the coolant is level with the lower edge of the filler orifice. Replace the filler cap.

> *Note.*—The exact amount of coolant required should be checked during the filling operation. If the correct filling level has been reached before the full quantity has been poured in, the presence of air locks in the system is indicated.

(vii) Run the engine at 1,500 r.p.m. for a period of about 30 seconds to circulate the coolant briskly and thus break down any small air pockets in the system.

(viii) Stop the engine as detailed in para. 36 of this Chapter.

(ix) Unscrew the filler cap, taking care to allow any pressure to escape before complete removal of the cap. Restore the level of the coolant and then replace the cap securely.

(x) It is emphasized that precautions must be taken against the splashing over of coolant and the consequent danger to personnel and deleterious effect upon the rubber-covered cables of the installation, the magnetos and the sparking plug screens.

(i) The approximate quantity of coolant required to fill the system is:—

3½ gallons, Spitfire aircraft.

(ii) The coolant used is of the same specification as that used in the main system and should pass through a fine mesh gauze filter before entering the system.

(iii) Remove the filler cap on the intercooler (or header tank) and commence filling the system with coolant.

(iv) The exact amount of coolant required should be checked during the filling operation. If the full amount cannot be poured in, air pockets are present and the engine should be given a short ground run to remove such pockets.

(v) Unscrew the filler cap, taking care to allow any pressure to escape before complete removal of the cap. Restore the level of the coolant and then replace the cap securely.

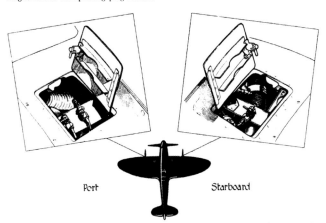

Port   Starboard

FIG. 4   LOCATION OF COOLING SYSTEM VENT COCKS – (SPITFIRE IX)

Intercooler cooling system

8. The intercooler system, which is entirely separate from the main cooling system, is filled through the filler cap orifice on the intercooler (or header tank). As in the case of the main system this orifice also determines the level of coolant in the system.

9. The following points should be observed when filling the system.

Draining storage oil from the carburettor

10. If the engine has been out of service, the carburettor will have been filled with oil for storage purposes and must, therefore, be drained by removing the base plugs (1), (2), (3), (4) and (5). In addition, the plug in the base of the air chamber should be removed to drain any moisture which may have accumulated in this chamber.

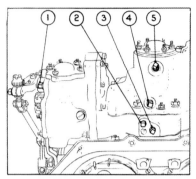

FIG. 5.—REMOVAL OF CARBURETTOR DRAIN PLUGS

Removal of the carburettor fuel filter

11. The carburettor fuel filter should be removed and cleaned. On replacement of the filter, ascertain that it is the correct way round, tighten the bolt securely, then lock the bolt with wire.

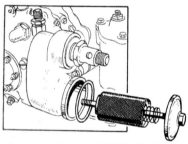

FIG. 6.—REMOVAL OF CARBURETTOR FUEL FILTER

Filling the carburettor

12. Whenever a carburettor has been out of use it is essential that it is primed with fuel. The vent plug must be removed to allow all air to escape from the fuel passages, otherwise complete filling of the system will be prevented.
Proceed as follows:—

   (i) Ascertain that the carburettor cut-off is in the CLOSED position.

   (ii) Remove the vent plug.

   (iii) OPEN the main fuel cock.

   (iv) Switch ON the auxiliary fuel pump until the fuel is level with the plug opening, then switch OFF the pump.

   (v) Replace and secure the plug.

Note.—A minimum period of 8 hours should be allowed for soaking the diaphragm with fuel, failing which, the carburettor functioning will be incorrect.

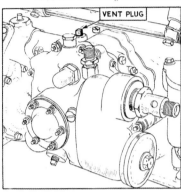

FIG. 7.—REMOVAL OF CARBURETTOR VENT PLUG

Initial priming of the carburettor after draining

13. If the carburettor has been drained, but is otherwise serviceable, it must first be filled as detailed in sub-para. (i) to (v) of the previous paragraph. After filling proceed as follows:—

   (i) Ascertain that the air-intake fuel drain is free from obstruction.

   (ii) Set the throttle lever half-open in its quadrant.

   (iii) Set the carburettor cut-off in the OPEN, i.e. forward, position.

   (iv) Switch ON the auxiliary fuel pump (or operate the wobble pump) and when fuel issues from the discharge nozzle, as indicated by fuel issuing from the air-intake drain, switch OFF the pump.

      Note.—After priming it is important to allow time for the fuel in the air intake to evaporate, otherwise difficulty in starting will be experienced.

Priming of the carburettor prior to starting

14. It is important to note that the procedure detailed in the previous paragraph must be strictly confined to initial priming and must not be used when it is required to remove air from the carburettor fuel passages prior to starting. For this latter operation, the following sequence is recommended:—

   (i) Set the carburettor cut-off lever in the OPEN position.

   (ii) Switch on the auxiliary pump (or operate the wobble pump) until the pressure warning light commences to flicker or goes out.

   (iii) Set the carburettor cut-off lever in the CLOSED position.

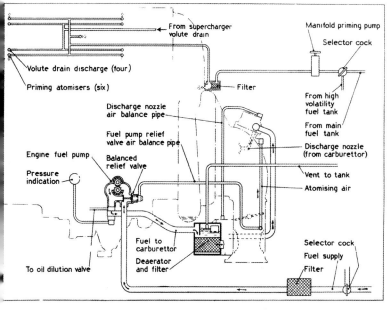

FIG. 8.—ENGINE FUEL SYSTEM

PRIMING THE INDUCTION SYSTEM

Turning and priming

15. The method of turning and priming simultaneously is considerably more effective than priming before turning, in conveying an explosive mixture into the cylinders for starting purposes, especially under cold weather conditions.

Priming a cold engine

16. The following tabulation relates to starting a cold engine and gives an approximation of the amount of priming that will be required for different atmospheric temperatures before the correct mixture is obtained within the cylinders and the engine may be expected to fire.

> Note.—If pre-heating apparatus is used, the engine will be appreciably warmer than the surrounding atmosphere and the temperature of the engine oil will provide a better guide to the amount of priming necessary in such cases.

Types of priming units

17. Varying aircraft installations may be fitted with either one of the following types of priming units.

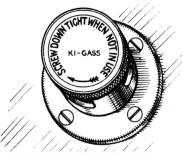

FIG. 9.—KI-GASS PRIMING PUMP TYPE B

(i) Ki-gass, Type B

Air Temperature	Approx. number of strokes required	
	100 octane (Stores Ref. No. 34A/75)	Special cold starting fuel (Stores Ref. No. 34A/111)
+ 30°C.	3	
+ 20°C.	4	
+ 10°C.	7	4
0°C.	12	8
− 10°C.		18
− 20°C.		

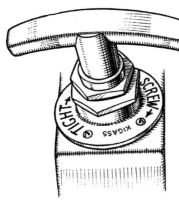

Fig. 10.—Ki-gass priming pump type k.40

(ii) Ki-gass, Type K.40

Air Temperature	Approx. number of strokes required	
	100 octane (Stores Ref. No. 34A/75)	Special cold starting fuel (Stores Ref. No. 34A/111)
+ 30°C.	1	
+ 20°C.	1	
+ 10°C.	1½	1
0°C.	3	
− 10°C.		2
− 20°C.		4

Priming a hot engine

18. The amount required under such conditions is small and it is recommended that first, an endeavour should be made to start the engine without priming.

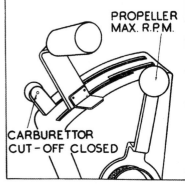

Fig. 11.—Position of engine controls before starting

SETTING THE CONTROLS FOR STARTING

19. Ascertain that the oil cocks (if fitted) are in the OPEN position and set the engine controls as follows:—

(i) The fuel system cocks in the ON position

(ii) The propeller control lever in the MAXIMUM r.p.m. position.

(iii) The throttle lever approximately half inch open to give 1,000 r.p.m

(iv) Retain the carburettor cut-off in the CLOSED position.

Note.—This control must always be set to the CLOSED position before the auxiliary fuel pump or the wobble pump is operated, otherwise the engine may be flooded with fuel.

STARTING THE ENGINE

20. The following sequence is recommended:—

(i) Switch ON the auxiliary pump (or operate the wobble pump) thereby priming the carburettor; the pressure warning light will go out when the required pressure is reached.

(ii) Operate the induction system priming pump until it is judged that the delivery line is full, as indicated by a sudden increase in the resistance of the plunger

(iii) Switch ON the ignition.

(iv) Press the starter and booster coil buttons and at the same time operate the priming pump while the engine is being turned (*see* para. 17 of this Chapter).

(v) When the engine fires, move the carburettor cut-off lever forward, i.e to the OPEN position.

(vi) Continued priming of the induction system *may* be necessary to assist the engine to pick up on the carburettor.

(vii) If the engine fails to continue running move the cut-off lever backwards to the CLOSED position

> *Note.*—If the engine fails to start it is important that the carburettor cut-off be secured in the CLOSED position and the auxiliary pump is switched OFF, before investigating causes of non-starting.

(viii) When the engine is firing steadily, release the booster coil button and turn off the priming cock and screw down the priming pump plunger.

Turning periods

21. These must not exceed 20 seconds limit with a 30 seconds wait between each attempt. Failure to observe this instruction may result in the battery plates being damaged or the starter brush gear becoming overheated.

> *Note.*—Under normal conditions the engine should start within 3 seconds.

Failure to start

22. If when the engine is turned with adequate speed, the engine refuses to start after four attempts, investigation should be made to ensure that:—

(i) The sparking plugs are firing efficiently.

(ii) The cylinders are correctly primed. Black smoke from the exhaust from intermittent firing indicates over-priming, while if the sparking plugs are functioning and there is no indication of a cylinder firing, under-priming is indicated. It should be ascertained that the priming nozzles are not choked.

(iii) For further possible causes of failure to start, *see* Chap. 3 of this Section.

STARTING UNDER COLD WEATHER CONDITIONS

23. The following precautions should be noted:—

(i) It will be found advantageous under cold conditions to turn the propeller several times in order to free the engine.

> *Note.*—All switches must be in the OFF position during this operation.

(ii) At temperatures below 0 deg. C. special cold starting fuel (Stores Ref. □ 34A/111), which is more volatile than the normal engine fuel is to be used, providing that the necessary priming connections have been fitted to the aircraft.

(iii) Prime the engine with diluted oil. Oil dilution should also be used before stopping the engine (*see* para. 38 of this Chapter).

> *Note.*—Oil dilution assures an adequate flow of lubricant to all moving parts of the engine at approximately normal working oil pressure and thereby permits easier starting and an earlier take off. Also the diluted oil in circulation reduces the possibility of bursting of flexible pipes and oil coolers when a cold engine is started.

24. After starting an engine in freezing conditions, it should not be shut down (unless this becomes necessary for any reason such as loss of oil pressure), until it has reached its normal working temperature

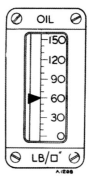

Fig. 12.—MINIMUM OIL PRESSURE GAUGE READING FOR GROUND RUNNING

PRELIMINARY RUNNING AND CHECKS

Oil pressure

25. This should build up to at least 45 lb. per sq. in. as soon as the engine is started. Under cold climatic conditions the indicated oil pressure may be temporarily much higher.

> *Note.*—Should the oil pressure be erratic or fail to build up under cold weather conditions, operate the oil dilution switch for a period NOT EXCEEDING ONE MINUTE.

Engine limitations
26. Run the engine at approximately 800 to 1,000 r.p.m. for half a minute or until the oil pressure is steady and then increase the r.p.m. to 1,200. Continue running at this speed until the oil inlet temperature is 15 deg. C. and the outlet temperature of the coolant is not less than 60 deg. C.

Oil pressure check
26(a). When the engine has attained its normal running conditions, an oil pressure check must be made. Set the throttle lever to give 2,650 r.p.m., when the oil pressure should not be less than 45 lb. per sq in.

26(b). It may be found, however, that in the case of an engine that has been run for a considerable time (and consequently has larger clearances than a new engine), or in the case of an engine that has been overhauled, that as the oil temperature rises the pressure may fall below 45 lb. per sq. in.

WARNING—The oil pressure must not be below 30 lb. per sq. in. when the oil temperature is 90 deg. C.

(i) *Engine running operational limits:*—These are laid down in Operational Limitations and must not be exceeded

(ii) *Propeller control lever.*—This must be in the maximum r.p.m. position except when the constant-speed unit is being checked.

(iii) *Boost pressure.*—High boost pressures must not be used for longer than is necessary for the check concerned and must never exceed +12 lb. per sq. in. on the ground.

(iv) *Cockpit throttle and propeller controls:*—These must be operated gradually and without snatch.

(v) *Prolonged idling.*—This should be avoided, since it causes fuel accumulation in the supercharger volute and, also, fouling of the sparking plugs tends to take place. These two features may eventually cause the engine to cut-out at take-off; it is important, therefore, that the engine should be speeded up periodically for

A 1300

FIG. 13.—MINIMUM OIL AND COOLANT TEMPERATURE GAUGE READINGS FOR GROUND RUNNING

Magneto preliminary check
27. When the engine has attained its normal running conditions, a preliminary check of the serviceability of the magneto must be carried out by switching off each ignition switch in turn. This ensures that, when other checks are being carried out, the engine will not be running on one magneto only, with consequent sooting up of the idle plugs and possible damage to the engine.

GROUND RUNNING PRIOR TO FLIGHT
28. The ground running prior to take-off must be kept at an absolute minimum to avoid overheating the engine. This applies particularly in the case of installations in which the radiators are not situated in the slipstream.

Routine checks
29. If the aircraft is normally in regular service, the complete checks need only be carried out once a day.

Note.—It is necessary however, immediately before flight, to carry out a power check and to ascertain that the engine gauge readings are within the approved limitations.

Precautions during ground running
30. The following precautions should be strictly limited:—

the purpose of clearing the volute casing of condensed fuel, by normal induction in addition to the slow-running suction device, and also for the purpose of clearing the sparking plugs.

DETAILED GROUND CHECKS
Two-speed supercharger
31. The change-over mechanism for the two-speed supercharger is automatic, being effected by means of an electro-pneumatic system which is operated by an atmospherically controlled aneroid. A test push-button is fitted to this control, enabling a check to be made when the

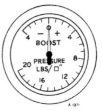

A 1371

FIG. 14.—BOOST GAUGE READING FOR SUPERCHARGER AND PROPELLER CHECKS

aircraft is on the ground. As this check is carried out at zero boost pressure, the boost control will then be inoperative and a slight variation in pressure may occur. The sequence of operations is as follows:—

  (i) Ascertain that the cockpit control switch is in the AUTO position (*see* fig. 2 of the following Chapter).

  (ii) Set the throttle lever to obtain ZERO lb. per sq. in. boost pressure. Operate the test push-button thereby setting the supercharger in high gear, whereupon a change in r.p.m., and possibly boost, will occur. The red warning light, indicating that high gear is engaged, will also come on.

  (iii) Release the push-button, whereupon low gear will be re-engaged, and the original engine r.p.m. and boost should be restored.

    Note.—It is necessary to ensure that a minimum air pressure of 150 lb. per sq. in. is available before carrying out this check as the operation of the gear change mechanism is dependent upon air pressure.

Propeller control

32. To check this control proceed as follows:—

  (i) With the propeller lever in the maximum r.p.m. position set the throttle lever to obtain ZERO lb. per sq. in. boost.

  (ii) Move the propeller lever from the maximum r.p.m. position until a drop of approximately 300 r.p.m. occurs. Return the propeller lever to the maximum r.p.m. position and check that the original r.p.m. are restored.

    Note.—Under cold weather conditions repeat this operation several times to circulate oil in the propeller hub.

Engine power

33. To check that the power output of the engine is satisfactory, proceed as follows:—

  (i) Ascertain that the propeller control is in the MAXIMUM r.p.m. position.

  (ii) Set the throttle lever to give +9 lb. per sq. in. boost pressure and note the engine r.p.m.

  (iii) At this boost pressure the propeller will be on its fine-pitch stops (i.e. it will behave as a fixed-pitch propeller), and as the total available power is used in maintaining it on the stops, any deficiency in power output will be indicated by a lower engine r.p.m. than is normally obtained at this boost.

Ignition system

34. To check the system, proceed as follows:—

  (i) Ascertain that the propeller control is in the MAXIMUM r.p.m. position.

  (ii) Move the cockpit throttle lever progressively to the take-off boost position. If rough-running occurs an ignition fault may be suspected.

  (iii) Throttle back to +9 lb. per sq. in. boost pressure and test each magneto by means of the magneto switches. The drop in engine speed should not exceed 150 r.p.m.

FIG. 15.—BOOST GAUGE READING FOR ENGINE POWER AND IGNITION CHECKS

Slow-running

35. Check the slow-running by closing the throttle suddenly from approximately 1,400 r.p.m. to idling speed. The engine should show no tendency to stop.

STOPPING THE ENGINE

36. When it is required to stop the engine, proceed as follows:—

  (i) Check that the propeller lever is in the MAXIMUM r.p.m. position.

  (ii) Allow the engine to run at approximately 800 to 1,000 r.p.m. for two minutes (with the aircraft headed into the wind, whenever possible), in order to clear and also to cool down the engine.

  (iii) Switch OFF the auxiliary pump, set the carburettor cut-off in the CLOSED position and at the same time open the throttle.

    Note.—It will be observed that the operation of the carburettor cut-off on these engines will stop the engine at any throttle position. The opening of the throttle, after operating the cut-off, ensures a clean cut-off without after-firing.

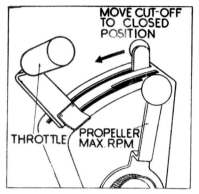

FIG. 16.—POSITION OF CONTROLS FOR STOPPING THE ENGINE

(iv) When the engine stops, switch OFF the ignition.

(v) Turn OFF the fuel cocks.

Inspection of engine oil filters

37. On completion of the initial ground run of engines that have been primed with diluted oil, filters must be inspected and cleaned. The use of diluted oil has a cleansing effect on the engine, with consequent accumulation of sludge in the filters, which, if not removed, may result in engine failure. This check must also be made after the initial flight test (*see* para. 24 of the following Chapter)

OPERATION OF THE OIL-DILUTION SYSTEM

38. In order to facilitate starting in cold weather, a system may be employed whereby fuel is added to the oil in circulation to reduce its

viscosity. By this means the torque required for turning when starting is greatly reduced. When therefore, it is known that the engine will be re-started under cold climatic conditions and with a cold engine, proceed as follows:—

(i) Stop the engine as stated in the previous paragraph.

(ii) Fill the oil tanks (if necessary), and if the engine is hot allow it to cool partially. To obtain the best results, the oil temperature should be between 10 deg. C and 45 deg. C. before dilution.

(iii) Re-start the engine and run up to approximately 1,000 to 1,200 r.p.m.

(iv) Operate the oil-dilution push-button in the pilot's cockpit.

(v) Continue running the engine with the oil dilution push-button in operation for a period NOT EXCEEDING ONE MINUTE, if the anticipated starting temperature (cold engine) is above --10 deg. C. When the starting temperature is expected to be below --10 deg. C. the dilution should be maintained for two minutes.

(vi) Stop the engine as stated in the previous paragraph before releasing the push-button, and check that it remains out after release.

(vii) Turn OFF the fuel.

39. If convenient, the benefit of dilution can be increased (particularly if the dilution has taken place at a high temperature) by allowing the engine to cool thoroughly and then re-starting and running at 1,000 to 1,200 r.p.m. for 30 seconds with the dilution push-button pressed. This distributes diluted oil to the cylinder walls and other normally hot surfaces from which it may have evaporated at the time of dilution.

40. After dilution, the engine can be left for two or three days during normally cold weather without the usual frequent running-up or re-dilution.

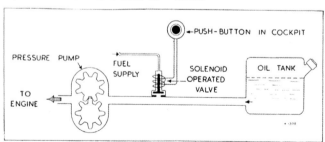

FIG. 17.—DIAGRAMMATIC LAY-OUT OF OIL-DILUTION SYSTEM

CHAPTER 2

IN FLIGHT

LIST OF CONTENTS

LIST OF ILLUSTRATIONS

OPERATIONAL LIMITATIONS

1. The operational limitations for the respective conditions of flight are stated in the front of this Volume.

Note.—These limitations, which cover engine speed, boost pressure, oil and coolant temperatures, together with the maximum permissible time limits where applicable, must be strictly observed.

Intensive flying

2. It is in the interests of reliability and engine life to keep well within the operational limits. For this reason, whenever possible, conditions less than those specified for maximum flying should be used.

TAXYING

3. When taxying, serious damage may be caused unless the following points are observed:—

(i) The minimum throttle opening necessary for the operation should be used.

(ii) If unavoidably heated, *before take-off,* allow the engines to cool to normal by heading the aircraft into wind and running the engine at a moderate r.p.m.

(iii) If the runway or dispersal point is uphill it is recommended that heavy aircraft should be towed rather than taxied into position.

OIL PRESSURE AND TEMPERATURE DURING FLIGHT

4. The oil pressure should not **normally** fall below 45 lb. per sq. in. at a maximum inlet temperature of 90 deg. C.

5. The minimum to which the oil pressure may be allowed to fall gradually is 30 lb. per sq. in. when the oil temperature is 90 deg. C.

Note :—This gradual fall in pressure may occur in the case of an engine that has been run for a considerable time (and consequently has larger clearances than a new engine) or in the case of an engine that has been overhauled.

5(a). Any sudden fall in oil pressure is indicative of either a faulty oil system or engine bearing failure. Similarly in the case of a sudden rise in oil temperature

Note.—If it is at all practicable, therefore, the aircraft should be landed at the nearest airfield and the cause of the trouble investigated.

MAGNETO CHECK DURING FLIGHT

6. It is important to check periodically that each magneto is working correctly. Failure of one magneto may not always be apparent during flight, as even though a fall in engine power will take place, the reduction would be insufficient to be indicated to the pilot.

OPERATION OF PROPELLER CONTROL

7. For taxying, take-off and initial climb, and combat flight, set the propeller control in the maximum engine r.p.m. position.

8. For climbing and cruising set the propeller control to maintain the engine speed within the appropriate limitations.

> *Note.*—When the propeller control is set to give approximately minimum r.p.m. the boost pressure must not be allowed to exceed that approved for cruising.

FIG. 2.—COCKPIT CONTROL FOR SUPERCHARGER GEAR-CHANGE

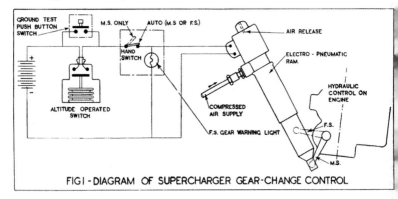

FIGI - DIAGRAM OF SUPERCHARGER GEAR-CHANGE CONTROL

CONTROL OF THE TWO-SPEED SUPERCHARGER

Automatic control

9. The change between low (M.S.) gear and high (F.S.) gear is automatic and is controlled by an aneroid switch, which at a pre-determined altitude closes a pair of contacts in an electrical circuit and energises a magnetic valve. The magnetic valve controls the supply of air to a pneumatic jack which on its outward stroke changes the two-speed gear from low to high. A return spring is provided in the jack which, on the descent of the aircraft and the breaking of the electrical circuit at the controlling altitude, retracts the jack and changes the two-speed gear to the low gear position. The aneroid switch makes contact at approximately 14,000 ft. (when the aircraft is climbing) to engage high gear, and breaks contact at approximately 12,500 ft. (when the aircraft is descending) to engage low gear.

Override control

10. An override control switch is provided, as shown in fig. 2, whereby the pilot may either retain the supercharger in low (M.S.) gear for the purpose of formation or other types of flying, or he may set the switch in the AUTO position and thus permit the automatic control to select the required gear as this becomes necessary.

TAKE-OFF AND CLIMB

Precautions before take-off

11. Before take-off it must be observed that:—

  (i) The propeller control lever is in the maximum r.p.m. position.

  (ii) The oil inlet temperature is not less than 15 deg. C.

  (iii) The coolant temperature is not less than 60 deg. C.

(iv) The engine oil pressure is not less than 60 lb. per sq. in. (*see* para. 4 of this Chapter).

> *Note.*—After running up and check testing, the aircraft should be taken off as soon as possible. If further idling is unavoidable, it should be done at 1,000 to 1,200 r.p.m. The induction system must be cleared just prior to take-off by speeding up the engine.

Control settings for take-off

12. The maximum permissible boost pressure is obtained by opening the throttle lever up to the gate. In the case of Spitfire aircraft, it will be found that a boost pressure less than maximum permissible will be sufficient for take-off.

> *Note.*—If the take-off r.p.m. is employed, it is necessary to re-set the controls when the aircraft has climbed to 1,000 ft. or within five minutes of leaving the ground, whichever provides the shorter duration of flight.

Control settings for climb

13. With the throttle lever set to obtain maximum climbing boost pressure and the propeller control lever set to obtain climbing r.p.m., the climb may be continued for one hour.

14. When a lower boost pressure than maximum for climbing is used, the automatic boost control is unable to open the throttle butterfly fully, and consequently, a gradual decrease in boost will take place as the aircraft climbs to full throttle height. Therefore, in order to maintain the desired boost, it will be necessary to advance the throttle lever progressively to the gate as the fall in boost takes place.

CRUISING

Maximum cruising boost and coolant temperature

15. If, when this boost pressure is used, the coolant temperature rises to the maximum permissible, the engine must be throttled back.

> *Note.*—It is permissible to use a temperature not exceeding 115 deg. C. for short period emergency; the boost pressure, however, must be reduced as much as possible.

Maximum engine life

16. To prolong the life of an engine it is essential to keep the power well within the limitations during a considerable proportion of the total flying time.

Maximum conditions for cruising

17. These constitute maximum Indicated Air Speed (I.A.S.) together with economical mixture strength.

> *Note.*—These conditions are distinct from the most economical cruising conditions at which the greater mileage per gallon of fuel is obtained (*see* the following paragraph).

Economical cruising

18. To obtain maximum range or to fly economically at any desired I.A.S., set the controls as follows:—

(i) The throttle lever to give a boost pressure not exceeding +7 lb. per sq. in.

(ii) The propeller lever to give an engine speed as low as possible within the cruising range, 1,800 r.p.m. min. to 2,650 r.p.m. max.

(iii) If, with an engine speed of 1,800 r.p.m., the power developed is more than that necessary to maintain the required I.A.S., adjust the throttle lever to reduce the boost pressure.

(iv) Conversely, if, with an engine speed of 1,800 r.p.m. and a boost pressure of +7 lb. per sq. in. it is not possible to obtain the required I.A.S., adjust the propeller lever to increase the engine speed to 2,650 r.p.m. maximum.

> *Note.*—For further information *see* the relevant Pilot's Notes.

COMBAT AND SHORT PERIOD EMERGENCY CONDITIONS

19. These conditions include climbing, diving, and level flight, and may be maintained for five minutes, subject to the boost and temperature figures not being exceeded, and an engine speed not exceeding 3,000 r.p.m. being maintained.

> *Note.*—It is emphasised that an overload is being imposed on the engine during these conditions.

20. It is pointed out that the fuel consumption at combat boost and r.p.m. will be increased by approximately 50 per cent. over the consumption at maximum climbing conditions and, therefore, that due consideration must be given to this increased consumption on the air endurance of the aircraft if the use of combat conditions becomes necessary during flight.

Fig. 3.—Position of engine controls for diving

Fig. 4.—Recommended setting of engine controls
for landing

DIVING

21. During all diving the throttle lever must be set at least one-third open in its quadrant. The propeller lever may be set at the cruising position. Normally the engine r.p.m. and boost in the dive will not exceed the combat maximum limitations.

Note.—A diving r.p.m. (*see* Operational Limitations), which is greater than combat r.p.m. is permissible for a period not exceeding 20 seconds limit.

LANDING

22. When approaching the airfield, the engine will be throttled back and the propeller control set to give climbing r.p.m.

Note.—If it is considered that the margin of power available is small, the propeller control must be set to give maximum engine r.p.m. as a precaution against an emergency.

STOPPING THE ENGINE AND OPERATION OF THE OIL-DILUTION SYSTEM

23. Full details of the correct method of stopping the engine and the operation of the oil-dilution system are contained in para. 36 and 38 of the previous Chapter.

FILTER CHECK TO BE CARRIED OUT AFTER FLIGHT

24. After the first flight of engines that have been primed with diluted oil or on which oil dilution has been carried out, it is essential that all the oil filters must be inspected and cleaned. This check must be carried out after a period of five hours' running or some such suitable period to suit Command requirements.

CHAPTER 3

RUNNING DEFECTS

LIST OF CONTENTS

LIST OF ILLUSTRATIONS

FAILURE TO START

The starting procedure detailed in Chap. 1 of this Section, used in conjunction with the experience gained by running a particular engine in varying climatic conditions, should enable the engine to be started easily. If difficulty is experienced, one or more of the defects outlined in the following paragraphs may be the cause:—

(i) Over-priming of the cylinders with fuel is indicated if the engine fires intermittently and black smoke issues from the exhaust when starting is attempted (*see* fig. 1).

    Note.—The best method of clearing the induction system is to switch OFF the ignition, open the throttles and turn the engine by the starter motor or by the hand-turning gear until the surplus fuel has been used. If it is possible to turn the propeller backwards by hand, this should be done after first turning the propeller in a normal direction to disengage the starter dogs. Repeat the starting procedure without further priming.

(ii) Insufficient priming of the cylinders is indicated if there is no sign of firing or if the engine backfires or spits while it is being motored. This may be caused by:—

    (a) Choked priming jets, atomizers, priming lines, or filter on the induction bend.

    (b) Leaking or broken priming pipes or connections.

    (c) Defective priming pump.

    (d) No fuel in the tank.

(iii) Faulty carburation or fuel system.

(iv) Faulty booster coil or ignition system.

(v) Defective starter system.

    (a) An exhausted or defective battery.

    (b) A defective starter motor or circuit.

IGNITION SYSTEM

Sparking plugs

(i) Deposits of lead on the electrodes.

(ii) Condensation on the electrodes.

(iii) Carbon or oil on the electrodes.

(iv) Incorrectly set plug gap.

(v) Cracked or broken insulation.

(vi) Incorrect type of plug.

Magnetos

(i) Pitted, dirty or unevenly seating contact breaker points.

(ii) Incorrectly set contact breaker gap.

(iii) Weak or broken contact breaker arm spring.

(iv) Sticking contact breaker arm.

(v) Dirty or worn distributor rotor and segments.

(vi) Faulty insulation on windings.

(vii) Magnetos incorrectly timed.

Ignition leads

(i) Faulty insulation of leads.

(ii) Faulty continuity (resistors missing).

(iii) Faulty terminals or connections.

(iv) Faulty isolating spark gap.

CARBURATION

Insufficient fuel supply

(i) Dirt under seat of fuel pump relief valve.

(ii) Incorrect adjustment of relief valve.

(iii) Faulty fuel pump diaphragm.

(iv) Obstruction in pipe-lines, filters, or tank vent pipes.

Excessive fuel supply

(i) Incorrect adjustment of fuel pump relief valve.

Flooding carburettor (engine standing)

(i) Carburettor discharge nozzle sticking in the open position.

(ii) Excessive fuel supply.

(iii) Failed diaphragm in carburettor.

(iv) Sticking air release float needle or mechanism.

(v) Carburettor cut-off set in OPEN position.

Weak mixture

(i) Insufficient fuel supply.

(ii) Air in carburettor fuel regulator.

(iii) Carburettor discharge nozzle sticking in closed position.

(iv) Restricted impact tubes or small venturi.

(v) Worn inlet valves or guides.

(vi) Air leaks in induction system.

Rich mixture

(i) Carburettor discharge nozzle sticking in open position.

(ii) Excessive fuel supply.

Momentary cutting during acceleration

(i) Air in carburettor feed regulator.

(ii) Defective accelerator pump valves or discharge nozzle.

(iii) Fuel building up in the supercharger volute (this is liable to happen after idling or during a prolonged glide).

AUTOMATIC BOOST CONTROL

(i) Aneroid valve overlap.

(ii) Damaged aneroid.

(iii) Incorrect adjustment of links or aneroid spring.

(iv) Sticking relay piston.

(v) Sticking aneroid valve.

(vi) Dirt in passages.

FIRING IN THE INDUCTION SYSTEM

(i) Very weak mixture.

(ii) Valves or valve seats dirty or pitted, resulting in the valve being kept open.

(iii) Valves incorrectly seating due to incorrect tappet adjustment.

(iv) Valve spring weak or broken.

(v) Valve stem or valve guide worn

(vi) Flame traps dirty or burnt.

(vii) Faulty ignition resulting in a retarded spark.

FIRING IN THE EXHAUST SYSTEM

(i) Faulty ignition.

(ii) Check the tappet clearances of the exhaust valves.

LUBRICATING SYSTEM

Low oil pressure

(i) Obstruction in pipe-lines.

(ii) Choked filters.

(iii) Dirt under seat of oil pump relief valve.

(iv) Incorrectly adjusted relief valve.

(v) High oil temperature.

(vi) Failure of a bearing.

(vii) Air leaks.

High oil pressure

(i) Incorrectly adjusted relief valve.

(ii) Low oil temperature.

Low oil temperature

(i) Faulty operation of radiator shutter

(ii) Faulty or incorrectly set viscosity valve.

High oil temperature

(i) Faulty operation of radiator shutter.

(ii) Damaged cooler resulting in internal restrictions.

(iii) External restrictions in radiator.

LACK OF POWER

The power output is indicated by the boost and r.p.m. registered and may be checked as stated in Chap. 1 of this Section. Lack of power may be due to one or more of the following causes:—

  (i)   Faulty carburation.
  (ii) Faulty ignition.
  (iii) Defective flame traps.
  (iv) Faulty compression.
  (v) Faulty propeller control mechanism.
  (vi) Overheating of the engine.
  (vii) Faulty boost control.
 (viii) Incorrect valve timing.

ENGINE VIBRATION

  (i)   Defective ignition system.
  (ii) Defective fuel system.
  (iii) Incorrect mixture.
  (iv) Defective propeller or control system.
  (v) Engine loose on mounting through:—
     (a) Loose holding-down bolts.
     (b) Deteriorated packings.
     (c) Loose bulkhead attachment.

    Note.—For the correct method of tightening the holding-down bolts *see* Sect. 3, Chap. 1.

OVERHEATING OF THE ENGINE

  (i)   Faulty operation of radiator shutter.
  (ii) Damaged radiator resulting in internal restrictions.
  (iii) External restrictions in radiator.
  (iv) Air-lock or restriction in coolant pipes.
  (v) Lack of coolant.
  (vi) Weak mixture.

MISCELLANEOUS DEFECTS

Surging
  (i)   Faulty automatic boost control.
  (ii) Faulty constant-speed unit.
  (iii) Faulty propeller mechanism.

Pre-ignition
This may be due to incandescent carbon within the cylinder or to incandescent sparking plug points arising out of:—

  (i)   Weak mixture.
  (ii) Retarded ignition.
  (iii) Faulty cooling system.

Irregular firing
  (i)   Faulty ignition system.
  (ii) Faulty carburation.

Detonation
This may be due to using a high boost pressure together with a fuel of low octane value.

GENERAL NOTES.   Exhaust flames will only be observed when an engine is running without an exhaust system or when stub pipes are fitted.   Flames will probably not be seen when flame-damping manifolds or exhaust ring collectors are used.   The types of flames shown will change as the air/fuel ratio is altered and will be affected by the presence of oil or corrosion inhibitor in the combustion chamber.

CORRECT MIXTURE STRENGTH.   A short light blue flame which may be almost invisible in strong light.

RICH MIXTURE.   A composite flame—short red-orange flame at the manifold, followed by an area of invisible flame, and terminating in an area of slow-burning gases bluish in colour.   If the mixture is very rich a black sooty smoke will be noticed and as the mixture strength is correctly adjusted the bluish flame will move towards the manifold.

WEAK MIXTURE.   Indicated by a fairly long bluish-white flame emerging directly from the manifolds.   The engine tends to back-fire at higher speeds.

WEAK MIXTURE AND BURNING OIL.   A reddish flame with a bluish tip and is one of the most commonly encountered, although it is sometimes confused with the red flame caused by burning oil.   This may be checked by moving the mixture control to the full rich position.   If the flame lessens, weak mixture and burning oil are indicated.

F.S/3.

Fig. 1.   PLATE I.   AERO ENGINE EXHAUST FLAME CHARACTERISTICS.

BURNING OIL. A short dull red flame usually accompanied by whitish or light grey, billowy smoke. This flame may be noticed in one set of manifolds but be entirely absent in another.

OVER PRIMING. Noticed only when starting. Intermittent thick, black billowy smoke, often followed by fire from the manifold. This type is caused by over priming, constitutes a dangerous fire risk and is detrimental to the engine.

DEFECTIVE SPARKING PLUGS. A very long whitish-orange flame appearing intermittently and inclined to be spasmodic or explosive in nature indicates detonation and may be due to defective sparking plugs. The flame usually appears from one or more manifolds.

INCOMPLETE COMBUSTION. An intermittent bluish-white, usually noticed when taking a magneto check. A drop in the r.p.m. may also be observed.

F.S/4.
Fig. I.   PLATE II.   AERO ENGINE EXHAUST FLAME CHARACTERISTICS.   (52-6345).

AIR PUBLICATION   1565 A

Pilot's Notes

PILOT'S NOTES

THE SPITFIRE I AEROPLANE

MERLIN II OR III ENGINE

Promulgated for the information and guidence of all concerned

By Command of the Air Council,

A.W.STREET

AIR MINISTRY

SPITFIRE I

May 1942
AIR MINISTRY

Amendment List No.25/J.
to
AIR PUBLICATION 1565A.
Volume I and
Pilot's Notes.

SPITFIRE I AEROPLANE
MERLIN II OR III ENGINE

Note: Amendment Lists to this Air Publication which
affect the Pilot's Notes are now allotted a
letter as well as a number. The letters will run
consecutively, omitting I and O. The Pilot's
Notes will be complete if the following "current"
amendment lists have been incorporated; these
have been allotted the letters shown:

13	14	18	19	25
A	B	D	F	J

---

(1) SECTION 2 — Para.5(iii)(b) Add at end of sub-para.: "The drop in r.p.m. should not exceed 150".

(2) SECTION 2 — Para.5. Mark end of this paragraph to refer to this sheet and note the following: "When engines are being kept warm in readiness for immediate take-off, de Havilland 20° C.S. propeller should be left in fine pitch - control lever fully forward".

(3) SECTION 2 — Remove existing sheets bearing Paras.10(iii) to 20(ii) and substitute new sheets supplied herewith.

(4) SECTION 2 — Remove Amendment List No.24/H and insert this sheet at end of Section as authority for the above amendments.

September 1941
AIR MINISTRY.

Amendment List No.18.
to
AIR PUBLICATION 1565A
Volume I and
Pilot's Notes.

SPITFIRE I AEROPLANE

MERLIN II OR III ENGINE.

Note:-   Amendment List No.17 affected Volume I but not
Pilot's Notes and was therefore not issued to
holders of the latter.

(31)	SECTION 2.	Para.1. (iii) Delete table giving r.p.m. and boost for cruising with weak mixture.
(32)	SECTION 2.	Para.4. (v) Alter to read "an interval of 15 seconds."
(33)	SECTION 2.	Para.5 (ii) (c). Delete "(2650-2700)"
(34)	SECTION 2.	Para.10.(iv) Mark to refer to this sheet and note that the speed quoted is that recommended for maximum range either level, climbing or gliding. (The optimum being 150 m.p.h. I.A.S.)
(35)	SECTION 2.	Para.14. (v) Delete "The Creeper - 80
(36)	SECTION 2.	Insert this sheet at end of Section 2

R.T.P/995. 4875. 9/41

October 1941.
AIR MINISTRY.

Amendment List No.19
to
AIR PUBLICATION 1565A
Volume I and
Pilot's Notes.

SPITFIRE I AEROPLANE

MERLIN II OR III ENGINE.

Note.-   The last Amendment List to this Air Publication affecting
Pilot's Notes was A.L. No.18.

(37)	SECTION 2.	Remove and destroy List of Contents.
(38)	SECTION 2.	Remove and destroy sheet bearing paras. 3 - 5 and 14 (ii) - 19 and substitute new sheets supplied herewith.
(39)	SECTION 2.	Renumber paras. 5 (ii) and (iii) to read 5 (iii) and (iv).

R.T.P/1014. 4875. 10/41

AIR PUBLICATION ....

Volume I

Pilot's Notes

AMENDMENT CERTIFICATE

Incorporation of an amendment list in this publication should be certified by inserting the amendment list number, initialling in the appropriate column and inserting the date of incorporation.

Holders of the Pilot's Notes will receive only those amendment lists applicable to the Preliminary Matter, and Sections 1 and 2.

Amendt. List No.	1	2	3	4	10	12	13	14	16	23
Prelimy. matter										
Leading Partics.										
Introducn.	✓									✓
Section 1		✓			✓			✓		
Section 2			✓	✓	✓	✓	✓		✓	
Section 3						✓				
Section 4										
Section 5										
Section 6										
Section 7										
Section 8										
Section 9										
Section 10										
Section 11										
Date of incorpn.										

INCORPORATED

MAR 1943

Amendt. List No.	244	25 J.							
Prelimy. matter									
Leading Partics.									
Introducn.									
Section 1									
Section 2	✓	✓							
Section 3									
Section 4									
Section 5									
Section 6									
Section 7									
Section 8									
Section 9									
Section 10									
Section 11									
Date of incorpn.									

NOTES TO OFFICIAL USERS

Air Ministry Orders and Vol. II leaflets as issued from
time to time may affect the subject matter of this publication.
It should be understood that amendment lists are not always issued
to bring the publication into line with the orders or leaflets
and it is for holders of this book to arrange the necessary link-up.

Where an order or leaflet contradicts any portion of this
publication, an amendment list will generally be issued, but when
this is not done, the order or leaflet must be taken as the overriding authority.

Where amendment action has taken place the number of the
amendment list concerned will be found at the top of each page
affected and amendments of technical importance will be indicated
by a vertical line on the left-hand side of the text against the
matter amended or added.   Vertical lines relating to previous
amendments to a page are not repeated.   If complete revision of
any division of the book (e.g. a Chapter) is made this will be
indicated in the title page for that division and the vertical lines
will not be employed.

Comments and suggestions concerning the subject matter of
this publication should be forwarded through the usual channels to
the Under-Secretary of State, Air Ministry.

LIST OF SECTIONS

(A detailed Contents List is given at
the beginning of each Section)

Introduction

R.T.P./443. 3000. 5/40.

SECTION I

PILOT'S CONTROLS AND EQUIPMENT.

INTRODUCTION.

1.   The Spitfire I is a single seat, low wing
monoplane fighter, fitted with a Merlin II
or III engine and a de Havilland 20° (P.C.P.)
or Rotol 35° constant speed airscrew.

MAIN SERVICES

2.   <u>Fuel system.</u>- Fuel is carried in two tanks
mounted one above the other forward of the
cockpit, and is delivered by an engine-driven
pump.
The tank capacities are as follows:-

Top tank:	48 gallons
Bottom tank:	37 gallons

The top tank feeds into the lower tank, and
the fuel cock controls (44 and 45), one for
each tank, are fitted below the instrument
panel.

3.   <u>Oil system.</u>- Oil is supplied by a tank of
5.8 gallons capacity fitted below the engine
mounting, and two oil coolers in tandem are
fitted in the underside of the port plane

4.   <u>Hydraulic system.</u>- An engine-driven
hydraulic pump supplies the power for operating
the undercarriage.

5.   <u>Pneumatic system.</u>- An engine-driven air
compressor feeds two storage cylinders for
operation of the flaps, brakes, guns and landing
lamps. The cylinders are connected in series,
each holding air at 200 lb/sq.in. pressure.

6.   <u>Electrical system.</u>- A 12 Volt generator,
controlled by a switch (60) above the
instrument panel supplies an accumulator
which in turn supplies the whole of the
electrical installation. There is an
ammeter (35) on the left of the switch.

Issued with A.L. No.14.

AEROPLANE CONTROLS

7. (a) <u>Primary flying controls and locking devices</u>.-
The control column is of the spade-grip (41)
pattern and incorporates the brake lever (40)
and gun firing control (39). The rudder
pedals (46) have two positions for the feet
and are adjustable for leg reach by rotation
of star wheels (47) on the sliding tubes.

(b) Control locking struts are stowed on the
right hand side of the cockpit, behind the
seat. To lock the control column, the longer
strut should be clamped to the control column
handle at one end and the other end inserted
in a key-hole slot in the right hand side of
the seat. The fixed pin on the free end of the
arm attached to this strut at the control
column end should then be inserted in a lug
(75) on the starboard datum longeron, thus
forming a rigid triangle between the column,
the seat and the longeron.

(c) To lock the rudder pedals, a short bar with
a pin at each end is attached to the other
struts by a cable. The longer of the two pins
should be inserted in a hole in the starboard
star wheel bearing and the shorter in an eyebolt
on the fuselage frame directly below the front
of the seat. The controls should be locked
with the seat in its highest position.

8. <u>Flying instruments</u>.- A standard blind flying
instrument panel is incorporated in the main
panel. The instruments comprise airspeed
indicator (29), altimeter (34), directional
gyro (37), artificial horizon (33), rate of
climb and descent indicator (36) and turn and
bank indicator (38). An air temperature gauge
is fitted on the extreme left of the instrument
panel.

9. <u>Trimming tabs</u>.- The elevator trimming tabs
are controlled by a hand wheel (7) on the left
hand side of the cockpit, the indicator (30)
being on the instrument panel. The rudder
trimming tab is controlled by a small hand
wheel (3) and is not provided with an indicator.
The aeroplane tends to turn to starboard when
the hand wheel is rotated clockwise.

10. (a) <u>Undercarriage control and Indicators (visual and audible</u>.- The undercarriage selector lever (78) moves in a gated quadrant, on the right hand side of the cockpit. An automatic cut-out in the control moves the selector lever into the gate when it has been pushed or pulled to the full extent of the quadrant.

(b) <u>To raise the undercarriage</u> the lever is pushed forward, but it must first be pulled back and then across to disengage it from the gate. When the undercarriage is raised and locked, the lever will spring into the forward gate.

(c) <u>To lower the undercarriage</u> the lever is pulled back, but it must first be pushed forward and then across to disengage it from the gate. When the undercarriage is lowered and locked, the lever will spring into the rear gate.

(d) <u>Electrical visual indicator</u>.- The electrically operated visual indicator (28) has two semi-transparent windows on which the words UP on a red background and DOWN on a green background are lettered; the words are illuminated according to the position of the undercarriage. The switch for the DOWN circuit of the indicator is mounted on the inboard side of the throttle quadrant and is moved to the ON position by means of a striker on the throttle lever; this switch should be returned to the OFF position by hand when the aeroplane is left standing for any length of time. The UP circuit is not controlled by this switch.

(e) <u>Mechanical position indicator</u>.- A rod that extends through the top surface of the main plane is fitted to each undercarriage unit. When the wheels are down the rods protrude through the top of the main planes and when they are up the top of the rods, which are painted red, are flush with the main plane surfaces.

(f) <u>Warning horn</u>.- The push switch controlling the horn is mounted on the throttle quadrant and is operated by a striker on the throttle lever. The horn may be silenced, even though the wheels are retracted and the engine throttled back, by depressing the push button (15) on the side of the throttle quadrant. As soon as the throttle is again advanced beyond about one quarter of its travel the push-button is automatically released and the horn will sound again on its return.

11.   Flap control.- The split flaps have two positions only, up and fully down. They cannot therefore, be used to assist take-off, They are operated pneumatically and are controlled by a finger lever (26). A flap indicator is fitted only on early aeroplanes.

12. (a) Undercarriage emergency operation.- A sealed high-pressure cylinder containing carbon-dioxide and connected to the undercarriage operating jacks is provided for use in the event of failure of the hydraulic system. The cylinder is mounted on the right-hand side of the cockpit and the seal can be punctured by means of a red painted lever (79) beside it. The handle is marked EMERGENCY ONLY and provision is made for fitting a thin copper wire seal as a check against inadvertent use.

(b) If the hydraulic system fails, the pilot should ensure that the undercarriage selector lever is in the DOWN position (this is essential) and push the emergency lowering lever forward and downward. The angular travel of the emergency lever is about 100° for puncturing the seal of the cylinder and then releasing the piercing plunger; it must be pushed through this movement and allowed to swing downwards. NO attempt should be made to return it to its original position until the cylinder is being replaced.

13.   Wheel brakes.- The control lever (40) for the pneumatic brakes is fitted on the control column spade grip; differential control of the brakes is provided by a relay valve connected to the rudder bar. A catch for retaining the brake lever in the on position for parking is fitted below the lever pivot. A triple pressure gauge (22), showing the air pressures in the pneumatic system cylinders and at each brake, is mounted on the left hand side of the instrument panel.

ENGINE CONTROLS

14.   <u>Throttle and mixture controls.</u>- The throttle
and mixture levers (16 and 14) are fitted in
a quadrant on the port side of the cockpit
and an interlocking device between them prevents
the engine from being run on an unsuitable
mixture. Friction adjusters (12) for the
controls are fitted on the side of the quadrant.

15.   <u>Automatic boost cut-out.</u>- The automatic boost
control may be cut out by pushing forward
the small red painted lever (17) at the forward
end of the throttle quadrant.

16.   <u>Airscrew controls.</u>- The control lever for the
de Havilland 20° or Rotol 35° constant speed
airscrew is on the throttle quadrant. The
de Havilland 20° airscrew has a **Positive Coarse
Pitch** position which is obtained in the extreme
aft position of the control lever, when the
airscrew blades are held at their maximum coarse
pitch angles and the airscrew functions as
a fixed airscrew. On early aeroplanes the
variable pitch airscrew is controlled by a
push-pull lever (9) on the left of the throttle
quadrant.

17.   <u>Radiator flap control.</u>- The flap at the outlet
end of the radiator duct is operated by a lever
(11) and ratchet on the left hand side of the
cockpit. To open the flap, the lever should
be pushed forward after releasing the ratchet
by depressing the knob at the top of the lever.
The normal minimum drag position of the flap
lever for level flight is shown by a red triangle
on the top of the map case fitted beside the
lever. A notch beyond the normal position in
the aft direction provides a position of the
lever when the warm air is diverted through
ducts into the main planes for heating the guns
at high altitude.

18.   <u>Slow-running cut-out.</u>- The control on the
carburettor is operated by pulling the ring
(50) on the right-hand side of the instrument
panel.

19. **Fuel cock controls and contents gauges.-** The fuel
cock controls (44 and 45), one for each tank, are
fitted at the bottom of the instrument panel. With
the levers in the up position the cocks are open.
Either tank can be isolated, if necessary. The
fuel contents gauges (72 and 77) on the instrument
panel indicate the contents of the top and bottom
tanks respectively, but only when the adjacent
push button is pressed.

20. **Fuel priming pump.-** A hand-operated pump (51) for
priming the engine is mounted below the right hand
side of the instrument panel.

21. **Ignition switches.-** The ignition switches (20) are
on the left hand bottom corner of the instrument
panel.

22. **Electric starting.-** The starting magneto switch
(68) is at the right hand bottom corner of the
instrument panel and the engine starting push-
button (53) is under a shield above the fuel cock
controls. Current for the starter motor is
normally supplied by an external battery, which
is connected to the socket on the engine mounting
U - frame, accessible through a door in the
engine cowling panel on the starboard side. The
general service accumulator carried in the aeroplane is also connected to the starter, but as its
capacity is small for such heavy duty it should
be used only as a stand-by.

23. **Hand starting.-** A starting handle is stowed behind
the seat. A hole in the engine cowling panel on
the starboard side gives access for connecting the
handle to the hand starting gear.

24. **Engine instruments.-** The engine instruments are
grouped on the right hand side of the instrument
panel and consist of an engine-speed indicator (61),
fuel pressure gauge (59), boost gauge (63), oil
pressure gauge (58), oil temperature gauge (62)
and radiator temperature gauge (65).

COCKPIT ACCOMMODATION AND EQUIPMENT

25. **Pilot's seat control.-** The seat (48) is adjustable
for height by means of a lever (80) on the right
hand side of the seat.

26.   Safety harness release.- In order that the pilot
        may lean forward without unfastening his harness,
        a release catch (76) is fitted to the right of
        the seat.

27.   Cockpit door.- To facilitate entry to the cockpit
        a portion of the coaming on the port side is hinged.
        The door catches are released by means of a handle
        at the forward end. Two position catches are incor-
        porated to allow the door to be partly opened
        before taking off or landing in order to prevent
        the hood from sliding shut in the event of a
        mishap.

28.   Hood locking control.- The sliding hood is provided
        with spring catches for holding it either open or
        shut; the catches are released by two finger levers
        at the forward end of the hood. From outside, with
        the hood closed, the catches can be released by
        depressing a small knob at the top of the wind-
        screen. Provision is made on the door to prevent
        the hood from sliding shut if the aeroplane over-
        turns on landing.

29.   Direct vision panel.- A small knock-out panel is
        provided on the right hand side of the hood for use
        in the event of the windscreen becoming obscured.

30.   Cockpit lighting.- A floodlight (13 and 67) is
        fitted on each side of the cockpit. Each is contro-
        lled by a switch (42) immediately below the
        instrument panel.

31.   Cockpit heating and ventilation.- A small adjust-
        able flap on the starboard coaming above the
        instrument panel is provided for ventilation of
        the cockpit. The flap is opened by turning a
        knurled nut underneath the flap.

32.   Oxygen.- A standard regulator unit (25) is fitted
        on the left hand side of the instrument panel and
        a bayonet socket (69) is on the right hand side of
        the cockpit.

33.   Mirror.- A mirror providing a rearward view is
        fitted at the top of the windscreen.

34.   Map cases.- A metal case (8) for a writing pad and
        another (4) for maps, books etc. are fitted on the
        left hand side of the cockpit. Stowage (74) for a
        height-and-airspeed computor is provided below the
        wireless remote contactor.

OPERATIONAL EQUIPMENT AND CONTROLS

35.(a) Guns.- The eight machine guns are fired pneumati-
       cally by a push-button on the control column spade
       grip. The compressed air supply is taken from the
       same source as the brake supply, the available
       pressure being shown by the gauge (22).

   (b) The push-button is surrounded by a milled sleeve
       which can be rotated by a quarter of a turn to a
       safe position in which it prevents operation of the
       button. The SAFE and FIRE positions are engraved
       on the sleeve and can also be identified by touch
       as the sleeve has an indentation which is at the
       bottom when the sleeve is in the SAFE position and
       is at the side when the sleeve is turned to the
       FIRE position.

36.(a) Reflector gun sight.- For sighting the guns and
       cannon a reflector gun sight is mounted on a
       bracket (31) above the instrument panel. A main
       switch (54) and dimmer switch (56) are fitted
       below the mounting bracket. The dimmer switch has
       three positions marked OFF, NIGHT and DAY. Three
       spare lamps for the sight are stowed in holders (64)
       on the right hand side of the cockpit.

   (b) When the sight is used during the day the dimmer
       switch should be in the DAY position in order to
       give full illumination, and if the background of
       the target is very bright, a sun-screen (57) can
       be slid behind the windscreen by pulling on the
       ring (55) at the top of the instrument panel. For
       night use the dimmer switch should be in the NIGHT
       position; in this position a low-wattage lamp is
       brought into circuit and the light can be varied by
       rotating the switch knob.

37.(a) Camera.- A G.42B cine-camera is fitted in the
       leading edge of the port plane, near the root end,
       and is operated by the gun-firing button on the
       control column spade grip, a succession of expos-
       ures being made during the whole time the button is
       depressed. When cannon are fitted the cine-camera
       is operated off the cannon-firing pipe line.

(b) A footage indicator and an aperture switch are
mounted on the wedge plate (10) above the throttle
lever. The switch enables either of two camera
apertures to be selected, the smaller aperture being
used for sunny weather. A main-switch (6) for the
cine-camera is mounted on the left hand side of the
cockpit.

NAVIGATIONAL, SIGNALLING AND LIGHTING EQUIPMENT

38. (a) **Wireless.**- The aeroplane is equipped with a
combined transmitter-receiver, either type T.R.9D
or T.R.1133, and an R.3002 set.

(b) With the T.R.9D installation a type C mechanical
controller (19) is fitted on the port side of the
cockpit above the throttle lever and a remote contactor (71) and contactor master switch (73) are
fitted on the right hand side of the cockpit. The
master contactor is mounted behind the pilot's
headrest and a switch controlling the heating
element is fitted on the forward bracket of the
mounting. The heating element should always be
switched OFF when the pilot leaves the aeroplane.
The microphone/telephone socket is fitted on the
right hand side of the pilot's seat.

(c) With the T.R.1133 installation the contactor gear
and microphone/telephone socket are as for the
T.R.9D installation, but the type C mechanical
controller is replaced by a push-button electrical
control unit.

39. (a) Navigation and identification lamps.- The switch
(24) controlling the navigation lamps is on the
instrument panel.

(b) The upward and downward identification lamps are
controlled from the signalling switchbox (66) on
the right hand side of the cockpit. This switchbox has a switch for each lamp and a morsing key,
and provides for steady illumination or morse
signalling from each lamp or both. The switch
lever has three positions: MORSE, OFF and STEADY.

(c) The spring pressure on the morsing key can be
adjusted by turning the small ring at the top left
hand corner of the switchbox, adjustment being
maintained by a latch engaging one of a number of
notches in the ring. The range of movement of the
key can be adjusted by opening the cover and adjust-
ing the screw and locknut at the centre of the
cover.

40. <u>Landing lamps</u>.- The landing lamps, one on each side
of the aeroplane, are housed in the undersurface of
the main plane. They are lowered and raised by a
finger lever (23) below the instrument panel. Each
lamp has an independent electrical circuit and is
controlled by a switch (32) above the pneumatic
control lever (23). With the switch in the central
position both lamps are off; when the switch is
moved to the left or to the right, the port or the
starboard lamp respectively, is illuminated.
A lever (18) is provided to control the dipping of
both landing lamps. On pulling up the lever the
beam is dipped.

DE-ICING EQUIPMENT.

41. <u>Pressure head heater switch</u>.- The heating element
in the pressure head is controlled by a switch (5)
below the trimming tab handwheels. It should be
switched off on landing in order to conserve the
battery.

EMERGENCY EQUIPMENT.

42. <u>Hood jettisoning</u>.- The hood may be jettisoned in
an emergency by pulling the lever mounted inside
the top of the hood in a forward and downward
movement, and pushing the lower edge of the hood
outboard with the elbows.

43. <u>Forced landing flare</u>.- A forced landing flare is
carried in a tube fixed inside the fuselage. The
flare is released by means of a ring grip (1) on
the left of the pilot's seat.

44. <u>First aid</u>.- The first aid outfit is stowed aft
of the wireless equipment and is accessible
through a hinged panel on the port side of the
fuselage.

Key to fig. 1

Port side of cockpit

1. Flare release control
2. Map stowage box
3. Rudder trimming tab control
4. Pressure head heating switch
5. Camera-gun master switch
6. Writing pad container
7. Elevator trimming tab control
8. Throttle and mixture friction adjusters
9. Push switch for silencing warning horn
10. Throttle lever
11. Mixture lever
12. Airscrew control lever
13. Connection for cine-camera footage indicator
14. Boost cut-out control
15. Landing lamp dipping lever
16. Landing lamps switch
17. Main magneto switches
18. Brake triple pressure gauge
19. Wireless remote controller
20. Clock
21. Elevator trimming tabs position indicator
22. Undercarriage position indicator
23. Oxygen regulator
24. Navigation lamps switch
25. Flaps control

27. Instrument-flying panel
28. Airspeed indicator
29. Artificial horizon
30. Altimeter
31. Direction indicator
32. Setting knob for (31)
33. Compass deviation card holder
34. Cockpit lamp dimmer switches
35. Brake lever
36. Landing lamp lowering control
37. Control column
38. Fuel cock lever (top tank)
39. Fuel cock lever (bottom tank)
40. Radiator flap control lever
41. Rudder pedals
42. Rudder pedal leg reach adjusters

Publisher's Note:
Due to the unavailability of original documents these cockpit views are taken from
the Spitfire II Pilot's Notes

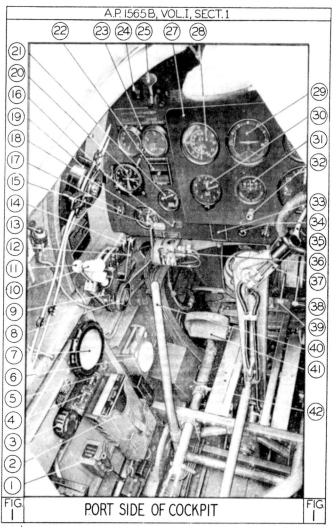

PORT SIDE OF COCKPIT

FIG. 1

FIG. 1

F.S./8

Key to fig. 2

Starboard side of cockpit

29.	Artificial horizon
31.	Direction indicator
34.	Cockpit lamp dimmer switch
38.	Fuel cock lever (top tank)
39.	Fuel cock lever (bottom tank)
43.	Brake relay valve
44.	Priming pump
45.	Compass
46.	Fuel contents gauge
47.	Engine starting pushbutton
48.	Turning indicator
49.	Rate of climb indicator
50.	Reflector sight main switch
51.	Reflector sight lamp dimmer switch
52.	Lifting ring for dimming screen
53.	Reflector gun sight mounting
54.	Dimming screen
55.	Ammeter
56.	Generator switch
57.	Ventilator control
58.	Engine speed indicator
59.	Fuel pressure gauge
60.	Spare filaments for reflector sight
61.	Boost gauge
62.	Cockpit lamp
63.	Radiator temperature gauge
64.	Signalling switch box
65.	Oxygen socket
66.	Wireless remote contactor mounting and switch
67.	Oil temperature gauge
68.	Engine data plate
69.	Oil pressure gauge
70.	Cartridge starter reloading control
71.	Height and airspeed computor stowage
72.	Control locking lug
73.	Harness release
74.	Slow-running cut-out control
75.	Undercarriage control lever
76.	Undercarriage emergency lowering lever
77.	Control locking lug

STARBOARD SIDE OF COCKPIT

FIG. 2

FIG. 2

A.P.1565A VOL.I SECT.2

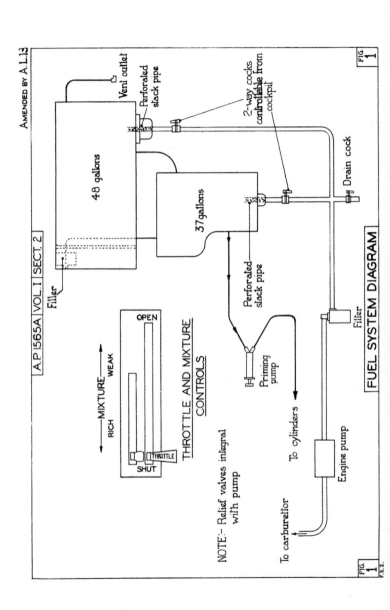

Vent outlet

Perforated slack pipe

Filler

48 gallons

2-way cocks controllable from cockpit

Drain cock

37 gallons

Perforated slack pipe

Priming pump

To cylinders

Filter

Engine pump

To carburettor

MIXTURE
← RICH   WEAK →

OPEN
THROTTLE
SHUT

THROTTLE AND MIXTURE CONTROLS

NOTE:- Relief valves integral with pump

FUEL SYSTEM DIAGRAM

FIG. 1

FIG. 1

F.S.2.

SECTION 2

HANDLING AND FLYING NOTES FOR PILOT

Note:- The flying technique outlined in these notes is
based on A.P.129, Flying Training Manual Part I,
Chapter III and A.P.2095, Pilot's Notes General,
to which reference should always be made if
further specific information is required.

1. ENGINE DATA : MERLIN II OR III

   (i) <u>Fuel</u>:-   Operational units: 100 octane only.
                Other units: 87 octane

  (ii) <u>Oil</u>:-   Key letter Y/Y.

 (iii) <u>Coolant</u>:- 30% Treated Ethylene Glycol. Stores ref.
                               33C/559.

  (iv) <u>The principal engine limitations are as follows</u>:

	R.p.m.	Boost lb/sq.in.	Temp. °C. Coolant.	Oil.
TAKE-OFF TO 1,000 FT.	3,000	$+6\frac{1}{4}$	—	—
CLIMBING $\frac{1}{2}$ HR LIMIT	2,600	$+6\frac{1}{4}$	120	90
CRUISING RICH	2,600	$+4\frac{1}{2}$	95	90
CRUISING WEAK	2,600	$+2\frac{1}{4}$	95	90
ALL OUT 5 MINS LIMIT	3,000	$+6\frac{1}{4}$	120	95

OIL PRESSURE: NORMAL: 60 lb/sq.in.
            EMERGENCY MINM (5 MINS):   45 lb/sq.in.

MINM. TEMP. FOR TAKE-OFF: OIL: 15°C.
                     COOLANT: 60°C.

   (v) <u>The following limitations must also be observed:</u>

      At +6¼ lb/sq.in boost: Minimum r.p.m. 2,080

      Diving: Maximum boost: +6¼ lb/sq.in.
                             Maximum r.p.m. 3,600

                3,000 r.p.m. may be exceeded only for
                20 seconds with throttle not less than
                one third open.

  (vi) <u>Fuel pressure:</u>   2½ - 3 lb/sq.in.

 (vii) <u>Combat concessions:</u>
      (a) When using 100 octane fuel, +12 lb./sq.in.
           boost, obtained by operating the boost control
           cut-out, may be used for short periods.
      (b) Maximum r.p.m. below 20,000 feet (½ hr.limit):
                                      2,850
           Maximum r.p.m. above 20,000 feet (½ hr.limit):
                                        3,000

      Use of these concessions must be reported upon
      landing and an entry made in the engine log book.

2.   FLYING LIMITATIONS

   (i) <u>Maximum speeds in m.p.h. I.A.S:</u>

      Diving: 450
      Undercarriage down: 160
      Flaps down: 140
      Landing lamps lowered: 140

3.   PRELIMINARIES

      On entering the cockpit check:

      Undercarriage selector lever - DOWN
                                     (Check that indicator
                                     shows DOWN: switch
                                     on light indicator
                                     and check that
                                     green lights appear).

      Flaps   - UP

      Landing lamps   - UP

      Contents of lower fuel tank.

4.   STARTING THEN ENGINE AND WARMING UP

   (i) Set:

Both fuel cock levers	— ON
Throttle	— $\frac{1}{2}$ inch open.
Mixture control	— RICH
Airscrew speed control	— Fully back.
Radiator shutter	— OPEN

  (ii) Switch ON the main and starting magnetos.

 (iii) Operate the priming pump to prime the suction
and delivery pipes. This may be judged by a
sudden increase in resistance of the plunger.

  (iv) Press the starting button, or begin hand
starting, and at the same time operate
the priming pump rapidly. The number of
strokes which must be given while the
engine is being turned, before it may be
expected to start, is as follows:

Air temperature °C.	+30	+20	+10	0	−10	−20
Normal fuel:		3	4	7	13	
High volatility fuel:				4	8	15

The engine should start without greatly
exceeding the above number of strokes, or
after not more than two if the engine is
hot.

January 1942.
Amended by A.L.No.24/H.

    (v) Turning periods should not exceed 20 seconds,
with an interval of at least 30 seconds
between each attempt.

  (vi) At temperatures below 0°C. it may be
necessary to continue priming after the
engine fires and until it is running
satisfactorily.

 (vii) As soon as the engine is running evenly,
switch OFF the starting magneto and screw
down the priming pump.

5.   TESTING ENGINE AND INSTALLATIONS

(i)(a) While warming up make the usual check of
temperatures, pressures and controls.

     Brake pressure should be at least
120 lb/sq.in.

  (b) See that the cockpit hood is locked
open and that the emergency exit door
is set at the "half cock" position.

 (ii) After a few minutes move the airscrew
speed control slowly forward and then
exercise it a few times.

(111)
(iii) After warming up, see that there are TWO men
on the tail and, with the airscrew speed control
fully forward, test as follows:-

(a) Open throttle to give zero boost and
check operation of constant-speed unit.

(b) Open throttle to give + $4\frac{1}{2}$ lb/sq.in boost
and check magnetos and oil pressure.

(c) Open up to full throttle momentarily and
check static r.p.m. (2650 - 2700) and
boost.

(iii)
IV Warming up must not be unduly prolonged because
radiator temperature before taxying out must not
exceed 100°C.

TAXYING OUT.

6.   It may be found that one wing tends to remain
down while taxying. This is due to stiffness in
the undercarriage leg, especially in a new aeroplane.

FINAL PREPARATION FOR TAKE-OFF - DRILL OF VITAL ACTIONS

7.   Drill is "T.M.P., Fuel, Flaps and Radiator."

T	- Trimming Tabs	- Elevator about one division nose down from neutral. Rudder fully to starboard.
M	- Mixture control	- RICH
P	- Pitch	- Airscrew speed control fully forward.

Fuel - Both cock levers ON and check contents of
lower tank.

Flaps   - UP

Radiator shutter   - Fully open.

F.S/5

TAKE-OFF

8.   (i)   Open the throttle fully. Any tendency to swing can be counteracted by coarse us of the rudder. If taking off from a small aerodrome with a full load, max. boost may be obtained by operating the boost control cut-out.

    (ii)   After raising the undercarriage, see that the red indicator light - UP - comes on (it may be necessary to hold the lever hard forward against the quadrant until the indicator light comes on).

  (iii)   Do not start to climb before a speed of 140 m.p.h. A.S.I.R. is attained.

CLIMBING

9.   For maximum rate of climb the following speeds are recommended:-

Ground level to 12,000 feet	185 m.p.h.	A.S.I.R.
12,000 feet to 15,000 feet	180 "	"
15,000 " " 20,000 "	170 "	"
20,000 " " 25,000 "	160 "	"

GENERAL FLYING

10.   (i)   <u>Stability and control</u>.- This aeroplane is stable. With metal covered ailerons the lateral control is much lighter than with the earlier fabric covered ailerons and pilots accustomed to the latter must be careful not to overstress the wings. Similar care is necessary in the use of the elevators which are light and sensitive.

    (ii)   For normal cruising flight the radiator shutter should be in the minimum drag position.

(iii) Change of trim.-

                 Undercarriage down   - nose down
                 Flaps down   - nose down.

 (iv) Maximum range: For greatest range fly in WEAK
mixture at 160 m.p.h. I.A.S. at the lowest
possible r.p.m.

  (v) For combat manoeuvres, climbing r.p.m. should
be used.

 (vi) For stretching a glide in the event of a forced
landing, the propeller speed control should be
pulled right back and the radiator flap put
at the minimum drag position.

STALLING.

11.(i) At the stall one wing will usually drop with flaps
either up or down and the machine may spin if the
control column is held back.

 (ii) This aeroplane has sensitive elevators and, if the
control column is brought back too rapidly in a
manoeuvre such as a loop or steep turn, stalling
incidence may be reached and a high-speed stall
induced. When this occurs there is a violent
shudder and clattering noise throughout the
aeroplane, which tends to flick over laterally and,
unless the control column is put forward instantly,
a rapid roll and spin will result.

(iii) Approximate stalling speeds when loaded to about
6,250 lb. are:-

                 Flaps and undercarriage UP   73 m.p.h. I.A.S.
                 "   "   "   DOWN 64   "   "

SPINNING

12.(i) Spinning is permitted by pilots who have written
permission from the C.O. of their squadron (C.F.I.
of an O.T.U.). The loss of height involved in
recovery may be very great, and the following
height limits are to be observed:-

    (a) Spins are not to be started below 10,000 feet.

    (b) Recovery must be started not lower than
        5,000 feet.

(ii) A speed of over 150 m.p.h. I.A.S. should be
attained before starting to ease out of the
resultant dive.

AEROBATICS.

13.(i) This aeroplane is exceptionally good for aerobatics.
Owing to its high performance and sensitive elevator
control, care must be taken not to impose excessive
loads either on the aeroplane or on the pilot and
not to induce a high-speed stall. Many aerobatics
may be done at much less than full throttle.
Cruising r.p.m. should be used, because if reduced
below this, detonation might occur if the throttle
is opened up to climbing boost for any reason.

(ii) The following speeds are recommended for
aerobatics:-

Looping.- Speed should be about 300 m.p.h. I.A.S.
but may be reduced to 220-250 m.p.h. when the pilot
is fully proficient.

Rolling.- Speed should be anywhere between 180 and
300 m.p.h. I.A.S. The nose should be brought up
about 30° above the horizon at the start, the roll
being barrelled just enough to keep the engine
running throughout.

Half roll off loop.- Speed should be 320-350 m.p.h.
I.A.S.

Upward roll.- Speed should be about 350-400 m.p.h.
I.A.S.

Flick manoeuvres.- Flick manoeuvres are not
permitted.

DIVING

13a(i) The aeroplane becomes very tail heavy at high
speed and must be trimmed into the dive in order to
avoid the danger of excessive acceleration in
recovery. The forward trim should be wound back
as speed is lost after pulling out.

(ii) A tendency to yaw to the right should be corrected
by use of the rudder trimming tab.

APPROACH AND LANDING.

14.(i) During the preliminary approach see that the
cockpit hood is locked open, and the emergency
exit door is set at half-cock position. Take care
not to get the arm out into the airflow.

  (ii) Reduce speed to 140 m.p.h. I.A.S. and carry out
the Drill of Vital Actions "U.M.P. and flaps".

        U - Undercarriage   - DOWN (Watch indicators
                                    and check green lights)

        M - Mixture control   - RICH

        P - Pitch   - Propeller speed control
                                    fully forward.

        Flaps   - DOWN

  (iii) When lowering the undercarriage hold the lever
fully forward for about two seconds. This will
take the weight off the locking pins and allow
them to turn freely when the lever is pulled back.
The lever should then be pulled back smartly to
the down position; if it cannot be pulled fully
back, hold it forward again for at least two
seconds. If it becomes jammed it may generally be
released by a smart blow of the hand. If this
fails it is necessary to take the weight of the
wheels off the locking pins, either by pushing the
nose down sharply or by inverting the aeroplane.
The lever can then be pulled straight back.

  (iv) If the green indicator light does not come on, hold
the lever fully back for a few seconds. If this
fails, raise the undercarriage and repeat the
lowering. If this fails also, use the **emergency
system** (see Section 1, Para.12.)

        Note: Before the emergency system can be used, the
control lever must be in the down position. It may
be necessary to push the nose down or invert the
aeroplane in order to get the lever down.

  (v) Correct speeds for the approach:-

        Engine assisted - about 85 m.p.h. I.A.S.

        Glide   -   "   90   "   "

F.S/7.

Amended by A.L.No.25/J.

(vi) Sideslips may be performed quite satisfactorily
with the flaps either up or down.

MISLANDING.

15.   Climb at about 120 m.p.h. I.A.S.

LANDING ACROSS WIND.

16.   The aeroplane can be landed across wind but it
is undesirable that such landings should be made
if the wind exceeds about 20 m.p.h.

AFTER LANDING

17.(i) After taxying in, set the airscrew speed control
fully back and open up the engine sufficiently to
change pitch to course.

(ii) Allow the engine to idle for a few seconds then
pull the slow running cut-out (if fitted) and hold
it out until the engine stops.

(iii) Turn OFF both fuel cocks.

(iv) When the engine has stopped, switch OFF the
ignition.

FLYING AT REDUCED AIRSPEEDS.

18.   Reduce the speed to about 120 m.p.h. I.A.S. and
lower the flaps. The radiator shutter must be
opened to keep the temperature at about 100°C and
the propeller speed control should be set to give
cruising r.p.m.

POSITION ERROR TABLE.

19.   The corrections for position error are as follows:-

	m.p.h.				I.A.S.				
From To	100 110	110 120	120 130	130 140	140 150	150 165	165 180	180 195	195 220	220 & over
Add Subtract	10	8	6	4	2	− −	2	4	6	8

FUEL AND OIL CAPACITY AND CONSUMPTION

20.(i) Fuel and oil capacities.-

Fuel capacity:-

2 Main tanks	-	top tank	48 gallons
		bottom tank	37 gallons
Total effective capacity			85 gallons

Oil capacity:-

Effective capacity   5.8 gallons

(ii) Fuel consumption:-

Max r.p.m.and boost for:	Height feet	Approximate consumption galls/hr.
Climbing	12,000	81
Cruising RICH	14,500	68
" WEAK	18,500	49
All-out level.	17,000	89
Most economical cruising (1700 r.p.m., 150 m.p.h. I.A.S.)	14,000	25

OIL DILUTION IN COLD WEATHER.

21.   See A.P.2095/4.   The dilution period should be:

Atmospheric temperatures above - 10°C: $1\frac{1}{2}$ minutes
Atmospheric temperatures below - 10°C: $2\frac{1}{2}$ minutes

AIR PUBLICATION 1565 J
Pilot's Notes

PILOT'S NOTES

SPITFIRE F.IX AEROPLANE

MERLIN 61 ENGINE

Prepared by direction of the
Minister of Aircraft Production

A. ⌐₁ Rowlands.

Promuligated by order of the Air Council

AIR MINISTRY

NOTES TO OFFICIAL USERS

Air Ministry Orders and Vol. II leaflets as issued from
time to time may affect the subject matter of this publication.
It should be understood that amendment lists are not always issued
to bring the publication into line with the orders or leaflets
and it is for holders of this book to arrange the necessary link-up.

Where an order or leaflet contradicts any portion of this
publication, an amendment list will generally be issued, but when
this is not done, the order or leaflet must be taken as the overriding authority.

Where amendment action has taken place, the number of the
amendment list concerned will be found at the top of each page affected,
and amendments of technical importance will be indicated by a vertical
line on the left-hand side of the text against the matter amended or
added.   Vertical lines relating to previous amendments to a page are
not repeated.   If complete revision of any division of the book
(e.g. a Chapter) is made this will be indicated in the title page for
that division and the vertical lines will not be employed.

R.T.P./1572.   2500.   10/42.

AMENDMENT CERTIFICATE

Incorporation of an amendment list in this publication should be certified by inserting the amendment list number, initialling in the appropriate column and inserting the date of incorporation.

Holders of the Pilot's Notes will receive only those amendment lists applicable to the preliminary matter, introduction and sections 1 and 2.

Amendt. List No.				4A						
Prelimy. matter										
Leading Partics.										
Introducn.										
Section 1										
Section 2				$\checkmark$						
Section 3										
Section 4										
Section 5										
Section 6										
Section 7										
Section 8										
Section 9										
Section 10										
Section 11										
Section 12										
Date of incorpn.				21/7/43						

Amendt. List No.											
Prelimy. matter											
Leading Partics.											
Introducn.											
Section 1											
Section 2											
Section 3											
Section 4											
Section 5											
Section 6											
Section 7											
Section 8											
Section 9											
Section 10											
Section 11											
Section 12											
Date of incorpn.											

AIR PUBLICATION 1565J
Volume I and
Pilot's Notes.

SECTION 1

PILOT'S CONTROLS AND EQUIPMENT

INTRODUCTION

1. The Spitfire IX is a single seat low wing monoplane
    fighter, fitted with a Merlin 61 engine and a
    Rotol 35° four-bladed constant speed propeller.

MAIN SERVICES

2. Fuel system.- Fuel is carried in two tanks
    mounted one above the other (the lower one is self-
    sealing) forward of the cockpit. The top tank
    feeds into the lower tank and fuel is delivered to
    the carburettor by an engine-driven pump. The
    tank capacities are as follows:-

Top tank:	48 gallons.
Bottom tank:	37 gallons.

    To meet the possibility of engine cutting due to
    fuel boiling in warm weather at high altitudes, the
    main tanks can be pressurised (operative above
    20,000 feet). Pressurising, however, impairs the
    self-sealing of tanks and should, therefore, be
    turned on only when the fuel pressure warning
    light comes on; this occurs at 6 lb./sq.in. In
    very warm weather at very high altitudes a rich
    cut may occur with the tanks pressurised and
    pressure must then be turned off. The aeroplane is
    fitted for carrying a long-range jettisonable fuel
    tank of 30 gallons capacity under the fuselage.

3. Oil system.- Oil is supplied by a tank 7.5 gallons
    capacity under the engine mounting, and two oil
    coolers in tandem are fitted in the under-side of
    the port plane. To prevent aeration of the oil the
    tank is pressurised by an automatic valve.

4. Hydraulic system.- An engine-driven hydraulic pump
    supplies the power for operating the undercarriage.

5. Pneumatic system.- An engine-driven air compressor
    feeds two storage cylinders for operation of the
    flaps, radiator flaps, supercharger ram, brakes and
    guns. The cylinders are connected in series, each
    holding air at 300 lb./sq.in. pressure.

6.   Electrical system.- A 12 volt generator, supplies
        an accumulator which in turn supplies the whole of
        the electrical installation.   There is a voltmeter
        (10) at the top of the instrument panel and a red
        lamp (40) to the left of the pilot's seat, marked
        "Power Failure", is illuminated when the generator
        is not charging the accumulator.

        AEROPLANE CONTROLS

7.   Primary flying controls and locking devices.-

    (a) The control column is of the spade-grip pattern
        and incorporates the brake lever and gun and
        cannon firing control.   The rudder pedals have
        two positions for the feet and are adjustable for
        leg reach by rotation of star wheels (45 and 57)
        on the sliding tubes.   Control locking struts
        are stowed on the right hand side of the cockpit,
        behind the seat.

    (b) To lock the control column, the longer strut
        should be clamped to the control column handle
        at one end and the other end inserted in a key-
        hole slot in the right-hand side of the seat.
        The fixed pin on the free end of the arm attached
        to this strut at the control column end should
        then be inserted in a lug on the starboard datum
        longeron, thus forming a rigid triangle between
        the column, the seat and the longeron.

    (c) To lock the rudder pedals, a short bar with a
        pin at each end is attached to the other struts
        by a cable.   The longer of the two pins should
        be inserted in a hole in the starboard star
        wheel bearing and the shorter in an eyebolt on
        the fuselage frame directly below the front of
        the seat.   The controls should be locked with
        the seat in its highest position.

8.   Flying instruments.- A standard blind flying
        instrument panel (6) is incorporated in the main
        panel.   The instruments comprise: airspeed
        indicator, altimeter, directional gyro,
        artificial horizon, rate of climb and descent
        indicator, and turn and bank indicator.

9.   Trimming tabs.- The elevator trimming tabs are
      controlled by a handwheel (30) on the left-hand
      side of the cockpit, the indicator (24) being on
      the instrument panel.   The rudder trimming tab
      is controlled by a small handwheel (27) and is
      not provided with an indicator.   The aeroplane
      tends to turn to starboard when the handwheel is
      rotated clockwise.

10.   Undercarriage control and Indicators.

   (a) The undercarriage selector lever (52) moves
       in a gated quadrant, on the right-hand side of
       the cockpit.   An automatic cut-out in the
       control moves the selector lever into the gate
       when it has been pushed or pulled to the full
       extent of the quadrant.

       A hydraulic valve indicator in the quadrant
       shows DOWN, or IDLE, or UP depending upon the
       position of the hydraulic valve.   UP or DOWN
       should normally show only when the selector lever
       is operated to raise or lower the undercarriage
       and IDLE when the lever has automatically sprung
       back into the gate after raising or lowering
       the undercarriage.   If, with the engine not
       running, the indicator shows DOWN, it should
       return to IDLE when the engine is started.

   (b) To raise the undercarriage the lever is pushed
       forward, but it must first be pulled back and
       then across to disengage it from the gate.
       When the undercarriage is raised and locked,
       the lever will spring into the forward gate.

   (c) To lower the undercarriage the lever is pulled
       back, but it must first be pushed forward and
       then across to disengage it from the gate.
       When the undercarriage is lowered and locked,
       the lever will spring into the rear gate.

   (d) Electrical visual indicator.- The electrically
       operated visual indicator (2) has two semi-
       transparent windows on which the words UP on a
       red background and DOWN on a green background
       are lettered;   the words are illuminated accord-
       ing to the position of the undercarriage.   The
       switch (34) for the DOWN circuit of the indicat-
       or is mounted on the inboard side of the
       throttle quadrant and is moved to the ON
       position by means of a striker on the throttle
       lever;   this switch should be returned to the OFF

position by hand when the aeroplane is left
standing for any length of time. The UP circuit
is not controlled by this switch.

(e) <u>Mechanical position indicator</u>.- A rod that
extends through the top surface of the main
plane is fitted to each undercarriage unit. When
the wheels are down the rods protrude through
the top of the main planes and when they are up
the top of the rods, which are painted red, are
flush with the main plane surfaces.

(f) <u>Warning horn</u>.- The push switch controlling the
horn is mounted on the throttle quadrant and is
operated by a striker on the throttle lever.

11. <u>Flap Control</u>.- The split flaps have two positions
only, up and fully down. They cannot therefore
be used to assist take-off. They are operated
pneumatically and are controlled by a finger
lever (5).

12. <u>Undercarriage emergency system</u>.- A sealed high-
pressure cylinder containing carbon-dioxide and
connected to the undercarriage operating jacks
is provided for use in the event of failure of
the hydraulic system. The cylinder is mounted
on the right-hand side of the cockpit and the
seal can be punctured by means of a red painted
lever (56) beside it. The handle is marked
EMERGENCY ONLY and provision is made for fitting
a thin copper wire seal as a check against
inadvertent use.

13. <u>Wheel brakes</u>.- The control lever for the
pneumatic brakes is fitted on the control column
spade grip; differential control of the brakes
is provided by a relay valve connected to the
rudder bar. A catch for retaining the brake
lever in the on position for parking is fitted
below the lever pivot. A triple pressure
gauge (25), showing the air pressures in the
pneumatic system cylinders and at each brake,
is mounted on the left-hand side of the
instrument panel.

ENGINE CONTROLS

14. Throttle control.- The throttle lever (33) is
     fitted in a quadrant, which is gated at the take-
     off position. There is a friction adjuster (31)
     on the side of the quadrant.

15. Propeller control.- The control lever (35) for the
     constant speed propeller is on the throttle quadrant
     and is moved forward to increase r.p.m. There is a
     friction adjuster (46) on the side of the quadrant.

16. Supercharger control.- The two-speed, two-stage,
     supercharger is automatically changed to S ratio at
     about 21,000 feet. On later aeroplanes an over-ride
     switch is fitted on the right-hand side of the
     instrument panel by means of which M ratio may be
     selected at or above this height. There is a push-
     button (42) to the left of the pilot's seat for
     testing the gear change on the ground, and a red
     lamp (13) on the instrument panel is illuminated
     when S ratio is engaged, on the ground or in flight.

17   Intercooler control.- The intercooler coolant
     system is automatic and M ratio is engaged if the
     charge temperature becomes excessive. This is
     indicated by the pushbutton (15) on the instrument
     panel which springs out; it may be reset by being
     pushed in. When the temperature of the charge
     returns to normal the pushbutton will remain in
     and allow the supercharger to return to S ratio.

18. Radiator flap control.- The radiator flaps are
     fully automatic and are designed to open at a cool-
     ant temperature of 115°C. They may be tested on
     the ground by pressing the pushbutton (41) to the
     left of the pilot's seat.

19. Slow-running cut-out.- The control on the carbur-
     ettor is operated by pulling the ring (37) below
     the left-hand side of the instrument panel.

20. Fuel cock controls and contents gauge.- The fuel
     cock control (47) for the main tanks is fitted
     below the engine starting pushbuttons and the
     fuel tank pressure cock (50) is below the right-
     hand side of the instrument panel. This cock
     should normally be OFF, but should be turned ON if
     the fuel pressure warning light (13) comes on. The
     cock control (58) and jettison lever (59) for the
     long-range tank are mounted together on the right-
     hand side of the cockpit, below the undercarriage
     control unit. The jettison

lever is pulled up to jettison the fuel tank but cannot be operated until the cock control is moved forward to the OFF position. The contents gauge (19) on the instrument panel shows the contents of the lower main tank when the adjacent pushbutton is pushed.

21.   Cylinder priming pump.- A hand-operated pump (48) for priming the engine is mounted below the right-hand side of the instrument panel.

22.   Ignition switches.- The ignition switches (1) are on the left-hand bottom corner of the instrument panel.

23.   Electric starting.- The booster coil (22) and engine starter (21) pushbuttons are fitted side by side at the bottom of the instrument panel. Each is covered by a safety shield.

24.   Hand starting.- A starting handle is stowed behind the seat. A hole in the engine cowling panel on the starboard side gives access for connecting the handle to the hand starting gear.

25.   Oil dilution.- A push-button (43) for operating the solenoid valve is on the left-hand side of the cockpit.

26.   Engine instruments.- The engine instruments are grouped on the right-hand side of the instrument panel and consist of an engine speed indicator (12), boost gauge (14), oil pressure gauge (20), oil inlet temperature gauge (17) and radiator outlet temperature gauge (16). The fuel pressure warning lamp (18) to the right of the contents gauge operates when the pressure drops to 6 lb./sq.in.

COCKPIT ACCOMMODATION AND EQUIPMENT

27.   Pilot's seat control.- The seat is adjustable for height by means of a lever (61) on the right-hand side of the seat.

28.   Safety harness release.- In order that the pilot may lean forward without unfastening his harness, a release catch (54) is fitted on the right-hand side of the cockpit.

29.   Cockpit door.- To facilitate entry to the cockpit
      a portion of the coaming on the port side is hinged.
      The door catches are released by means of a handle
      (29) at the forward end. Two-position catches are
      incorporated to allow the door to be partly opened
      before taking off or landing in order to prevent
      the hood from sliding shut in the event of a mishap.

30.   Hood locking control.- The sliding hood is provided
      with spring catches for holding it either open or
      shut;   the catches are released by two finger levers
      at the forward end of the hood. From outside, with
      the hood closed, the catches can be released by
      depressing a small knob at the top of the windscreen.
      Provision is made on the door to prevent the hood
      from sliding shut if the aeroplane overturns on
      landing.

31.   Direct vision panel.- A small knock-out panel is
      provided on the right-hand side of the hood for
      use in the event of the windscreen becoming
      obscured.

32.   Cockpit lighting.- A floodlight (32) is fitted on
      each side of the cockpit. Each is controlled by a
      switch (23) on the instrument panel.

33.   Cockpit heating and ventilation.- A small adjust-
      able flap on the starboard coaming above the
      instrument panel is provided for ventilation of
      the cockpit. The flap is opened by turning a
      knurled nut (11) underneath the flap.

34.   Oxygen.- A standard regulator unit (3) is fitted
      on the left-hand side of the instrument panel and
      a bayonet socket is on the right-hand side of the
      cockpit. A separate cock (65) is provided in
      addition to the regulator.

35.   Mirror.- A mirror providing a rearward view is
      fitted at the top of the windscreen.

36.   Map cases.- A metal case (44) for maps, books etc.
      is fitted on the left-hand side of the cockpit.
      Stowage for a height-and-airspeed computor is
      provided below the wireless remote contactor.

        OPERATIONAL EQUIPMENT AND CONTROLS

37.   Guns and Cannon.- The machine guns and cannon are
      fired pneumatically by means of a triple push-

button on the control column spade grip. The compressed air supply is taken from the same source as the brake supply, the available pressure being shown by the gauge. The push-button is fitted with a milled finger which extends out of the bottom and is a means of locking the button in the SAFE position, SAFE and FIRE being engraved on the adjacent casing. When the catch is in the FIRE position, a pip also extends out of the top of the casing so that the pilot can ascertain by feel the setting of the push-button.

38.   **Reflector gun sight.-** For sighting the guns and cannon a reflector gun sight (9) is mounted on a bracket above the instrument panel. A main switch (8) and dimmer switch are fitted below the mounting bracket. The dimmer switch has three positions marked OFF, NIGHT and DAY. Three spare lamps for the sight are stowed in holders on the right-hand side of the cockpit. When the sight is used during the day the dimmer switch should be in the DAY position in order to give full illumination, and if the background of the target is very bright, a sun-screen can be slid behind the windscreen by pulling on the ring (7) at the top of the instrument panel. For night use the dimmer switch should be in the NIGHT position; in this position a low-wattage lamp is brought into circuit and the lights can be varied by rotating the switch knob.

NAVIGATIONAL, SIGNALLING AND LIGHTING EQUIPMENT

39.   **Wireless.-** The aeroplane is equipped with a type T.R.1133 combined transmitter-receiver and an R.3002 or R.3060 set. The pushbutton electrical control unit (36) for the T.R.1133 set is on the left-hand side of the cockpit above the throttle quadrant, and a remote contactor (51) and contactor master switch are fitted on the right-hand side of the cockpit. The master contactor is mounted behind the pilot's headrest and a switch controlling the heating element is fitted on the forward bracket of the mounting. The heating element should always be switched OFF when the pilot leaves the aeroplane. The microphone/telephone socket (64) is fitted on the right-hand side of the pilot's seat. The R.3002 or R.3060 push-buttons (53) are on the right-hand side of the cockpit, and the master switch (55) immediately aft of these.

40.   **Navigation and identification lamps.-** The switch
      (4) controlling the navigation lamps is on the
      instrument panel. The upward and downward identi-
      fication lamps are controlled from the signalling
      switchbox (49) on the right-hand side of the cock-
      pit. This switchbox has a switch for each lamp
      and a morsing key, and provides for steady illumin-
      ation or morse signalling from each lamp or both.
      The switch lever has three positions: MORSE, OFF
      and STEADY. The spring pressure on the morsing
      key can be adjusted by turning the small ring at
      the top left-hand corner of the switchbox, adjust-
      ment being maintained by a latch engaging one of
      a number of notches in the ring. The range of
      movement of the key can be adjusted by opening
      the cover and adjusting the screw and locknut at
      the centre of the cover.

41.   **Signal discharger.-**

   (a) The recognition device, which fires a cartridge
       out of the top of the rear fuselage, is operated
       by giving an upward pull of the handle (39) which
       is fitted on the left of the pilot's seat. Upon
       release, the handle will return to the normal
       position on its own accord. On no account should
       it be pushed back to normal as this may cause damage
       to the cable, resulting in the control becoming
       inoperative.

   (b) A pre-selector control (38) is fitted immediately
       above the handle, by means of which one of various
       cartridges may be selected before firing.

      DE-ICING EQUIPMENT

42.   **Windscreen de-icing.-**

      A tank containing the de-icing solution is mounted
      on the right-hand side of the cockpit directly
      above the bottom longeron. A cock (60) is mounted
      above the tank, and a pump (63) and a needle valve
      (62) to control the flow of the liquid are mounted
      below the undercarriage emergency lowering control.
      Liquid is pumped from the tank to a spray at the
      base of the windscreen, from which it is sprayed
      over the front panel of the screen. The flow of
      liquid is governed by the needle valve, after turn-
      ing ON the cock and pushing down the pump plunger
      to its full extent.

The plunger will return to the extended position on its own, and if required, it can be pushed down again. When de-icing is no longer required the cock should be turned to the OFF position.

43.   Pressure head heater switch.- The heating element in the pressure head is controlled by a switch (28) just forward of the rudder trimming tab handwheel.

EMERGENCY EQUIPMENT

44.   Hood jettisoning.- The hood may be jettisoned in an emergency by pulling the lever mounted inside the top of the hood in a forward and downward movement, and pushing the lower edge of the hood outboard with the elbows. A crowbar (26) for use in an emergency, is stowed on the inside of the door.

45.   First-aid.- The first-aid outfit is stowed aft of the wireless equipment and is accessible through a hinged panel on the port side of the fuselage.

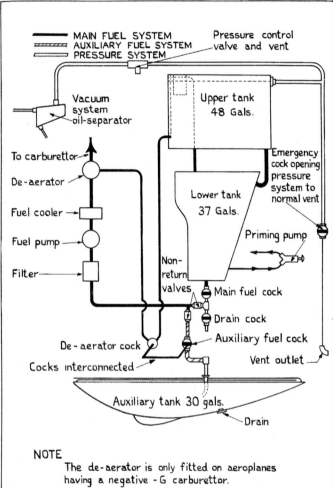

MAIN FUEL SYSTEM
AUXILIARY FUEL SYSTEM
PRESSURE SYSTEM

Pressure control valve and vent

Vacuum system oil-separator

Upper tank 48 Gals.

To carburettor

De-aerator

Fuel cooler

Fuel pump

Filter

Lower tank 37 Gals.

Emergency cock opening pressure system to normal vent

Priming pump

Non-return valves

Main fuel cock

Drain cock

De-aerator cock

Auxiliary fuel cock

Cocks interconnected

Vent outlet

Auxiliary tank 30 gals.

Drain

NOTE

The de-aerator is only fitted on aeroplanes having a negative - G carburettor.

FIG 4   FUEL SYSTEM DIAGRAM   FIG 4

SECTION 2
HANDLING AND FLYING NOTES FOR PILOT

Note: The flying technique outlined in these notes is
based on A.P.129, Flying Training Manual Part I,
Chapter III, and A.P.2095, Pilot's Notes General,
to which reference should always be made if further
information is required.

1.   ENGINE DATA: MERLIN 61.

   (i) Fuel   100 octane only.

  (ii) Oil: See A.P.1464/C.37.

 (iii) Engine limitations:

		R.p.m.	Boost lb/sq.in.	Temp. Coolant	°C Oil.
MAX. TAKE-OFF TO 1,000 FEET	M	3,000	+12	135	-
MAX. CLIMBING ½ HR LIMIT	M	2,850	+12	125	90
	S	2,850	+12	125	90
MAX. RICH CONTINUOUS	M	2,650	+ 7	105	90
	S	2,650	+ 7	105	90
MAX.ECONOMICAL CONTINUOUS	M	2,650	+ 4	105	90
	S	2,650	+ 4	105	90
MAX. ALL OUT 5 MINS LIMIT	M	3,000	+15	125	95
	S	3,000	+15	125	95

OIL PRESSURE: NORMAL: 60 lb./sq.in.
                 EMERGENCY MINM. (5 MINS): 45 lb./sq.in.

MINM. TEMP. FOR TAKE-OFF: OIL: 15°C.
                            COOLANT: 60°C.

  (iv) Fuel pressure: 8 - 10 lb./sq.in.

2.   POSITION ERROR CORRECTIONS

From To	135 150	150 165	165 185	185 205	205 225	225 250	250 280	280 320	m.p.h.I.A.S. m.p.h.I.A.S.
Add	6	4	2	-	-	-	-	-	m.p.h.
Subtract	-	-	-	-	2	4	6	8	m.p.h.

3.   FLYING LIMITATIONS

The aeroplane is designed for the following speeds:

    Diving: 450 m.p.h. I.A.S.
    Undercarriage down: 160 m.p.h. I.A.S.
    Flaps down: 160 m.p.h. I.A.S.

4.   MANAGEMENT OF FUEL SYSTEM

When fitted with a jettisonable fuel tank:

   (i) Start and warm up in the normal way on the main
       tanks.

  (ii) Take-off on the main tanks and change over to the
       jettisonable tank at a safe height (say 2,000 feet).
       Turn OFF the main tanks.

 (iii) Normally the aeroplane should be flown on the
       jettisonable tank until the fuel is exhausted.
       When the engine cuts turn ON the main tanks and
       turn OFF the jettisonable tank at once.

  (iv) If the tank is to be jettisoned before the fuel in
       it is exhausted, first turn ON the main tanks and
       then move the jettisonable tank cock control to OFF
       before operating the jettison lever.

       Note: The jettisonable tank cock must be kept OFF
             when the tank is jettisoned or when the fuel
             in it is exhausted, otherwise air may be
             sucked into the main fuel system. The tank
             should be jettisoned only in straight and
             level flight.

5.   PRELIMINARIES

   (i) Check contents of lower fuel tank. If fitted with
       a jettisonable fuel tank see that cock is OFF.

(11) Check that undercarriage lever is DOWN. Switch on indicator and see that DOWN shows green.

6.   STARTING ENGINES AND WARMING UP

(1) Set fuel cock lever ON.

(11) Set the controls as follows:

Throttle   - $\frac{1}{4}$ inch open
Propeller control   - Fully forward.

(iii) High volatility fuel (Stores ref. 34A/111) should be used if possible for priming at air temperatures below freezing. Work the priming pump until the fuel reaches the priming nozzles; this may be judged by a sudden increase in resistance.

(iv) Switch ON the ignition and press the starter and booster coil buttons. Turning periods must not exceed 20 seconds, with a 30 seconds wait between each. Work the priming pump as rapidly and vigorously as possible while the engine is being turned; it should start after the following number of strokes if cold:

Air temperature °C:	+30	+20	+10	0	-10	-20
Normal fuel:		3	4	7	12	
H.V. fuel:				4	8	18

(v) At temperatures below freezing it will probably be necessary to continue priming after the engine has fired and until it picks up on the carburettor.

(vi) As soon as the engine is running satisfactorily, release the booster coil button and screw down the priming pump.

(vii) Run the engine as slowly as possible for half a minute, then warm up at a fast tick-over.

7.   TESTING ENGINES AND INSTALLATIONS

While warming up:

(1) Check temperatures and pressures, and test operation of the controls.

(ii) Press the radiator test push-button and have ground
crew check that shutters open.

After warming up, with ~~two~~ *three* men on the tail: AND ONE
ON THE STARBOARD WING-TIP.   A.L.

(iii) Open up to maximum economical continuous boost;
exercise and check operation of the two-speed
supercharger. R.p.m. should fall when S ratio
is engaged and the red light should come on.

(iv) At maximum economical continuous boost exercise
and check operation of the constant speed propeller. R.p.m. should fall to 1,800 with the
control fully back.

(v) Open the throttle to the gate and check take-off
boost and static r.p.m., which should be 3,000 at
take-off boost.

(vi) Throttle back to maximum rich continuous boost and
test each magneto in turn. The drop should not
exceed 150 r.p.m.

(vii) Before taxying check brake pressure (120 lb./sq.in.)
and machine gun and cannon firing pressure (220 lb.
/sq.in.).

8.   FINAL PREPARATIONS FOR TAKE-OFF

The Drill of Vital Actions is T,P,Fuel, Flaps and
Supercharger:

T	-	Trimming tabs	- Elevator: neutral to half a division nose down. Rudder: fully to starboard.
P	-	Propeller control	- Fully forward.
		Fuel	- Check contents of lower tank. Main tank cock ON. Jettisonable tank cock OFF.
		Flaps	- UP
		Supercharger	- Over-ride switch up.

9.   TAKE-OFF

   (i) Open the throttle slowly to the gate.

   (ii) Any tendency to swing can be counteracted by
        the rudder.

   (iii) After raising the undercarriage, see that the red
         indicator light -UP- comes on. It may be necessary
         to hold the lever hard forward against the quadrant
         until the indicator light comes on.

   (iv) Do not start to climb before a speed of 140 m.p.h.
        I.A.S. is attained.

10.   CLIMBING

   (i) The speeds for maximum rate of climb are as
       follows:

       Up to 25,000 feet: 160 m.p.h. I.A.S.
       At   30,000 feet: 145 m.p.h. I.A.S.
       At   35,000 feet: 130 m.p.h. I.A.S.
       At   40,000 feet: 115 m.p.h. I.A.S.

       For intermediate heights, reduce speed by 3 m.p.h.
       per 1,000 feet.

   (ii) At high altitudes the true forward speed on the
        climb is exceptionally high; for example, at
        40,000 feet the speed for maximum rate of climb is
        115 m.p.h. I.A.S; 230 m.p.h. true.

   (iii) The fuel tank pressure cock should normally be kept
         OFF, but should be turned ON if the fuel pressure
         warning light comes on. (This indicates that
         pressure has dropped to 6 lb/sq.in.).

11.   ECONOMICAL CRUISING

   (i) For maximum range fly at 2,000 r.p.m. and +4 lb/
       sq.in. boost (if obtainable). The limit of +4 lb/
       sq.in. should be observed, as the mixture is auto-
       matically richened at boosts in excess of this.
       Accept whatever I.A.S. these engine conditions give,
       provided that it is above 170 m.p.h. I.A.S. If
       speed falls below 170 m.p.h. I.A.S., increase r.p.m.

   (ii) For maximum range and endurance the jettisonable
        fuel tank (if fitted) should be jettisoned as soon
        as it is empty.

12.   FUEL CONSUMPTION

The approximate fuel consumptions (gals/hr) are
as follows:

(i) Weak mixture (as obtained at +4 lb/sq.in. boost
                                        and below):

Boost lb/sq.in.	R.P.M.				
	2,650	2,400	2,200	2,000	1,800
+4	71	66	61	54	-
+2	66	61	57	50	43
0	60	55	51	45	39
-2	53	49	45	40	35
-4	45	42	38	34	30

(ii) Rich mixture (as obtained above +4 lb/sq.in. boost):

Boost lb/sq.in.	R.P.M.	gals/hr.
+15	3,000	130
+12	2,850	105
+ 7	2,650	80

13.   FUEL CAPACITY

Top tank:	48 gallons
Bottom tank:	37 gallons
Normal capacity:	85 gallons
Long-range tank (if fitted):	30 gallons
Total long-range capacity:	115 gallons

14.   GENERAL FLYING

(i) Stability: Longitudinal stability is somewhat
better than on earlier Marks.

(ii) Change of trim:

Undercarriage down	-	Nose down
Flaps down	-	Nose down

(iii) The aircraft is slightly heavier on the elevator
than earlier Marks.

(iv) In bad visibility near the ground flaps should be
lowered and the propeller set to give cruising
r.p.m. Speed may then be reduced to 130 m.p.h.
I.A.S.

(v) For stretching a glide in the event of a forced
landing, the propeller speed control should be
pulled right back.

15.   STALLING

The stalling speeds (engine off) in m.p.h. I.A.S.
are:
    Undercarriage and flaps up: 86
    Undercarriage and flaps down: 76

16.   SPINNING

Spinning is not permitted.

17.   AEROBATICS

(i) Flick manoeuvres are not permitted.

(ii) The following speeds (m.p.h. I.A.S.) are recommended:

    Loop: 280 - 300
    Roll: 220 - 300
    Half roll off loop: 320 - 350
    Upward roll: 350 - 400

18.   DIVING

(i) The aeroplane should be trimmed into and out of the
dive.

(ii) A tendency to yaw to starboard should be corrected
by use of the rudder trimming tab.

19.   APPROACH AND LANDING

(i) Check brake pressure (120 lb./sq.in.).

(ii) Reduce speed to 140 m.p.h. I.A.S. and carry out the
Drill of Vital Actions U,P, Supercharger and Flaps:

U - Undercarriage   - DOWN

P - Propeller control   - Fully forward.

Supercharger   - Over-ride switch up.

Flaps   - DOWN.

(iii) Approach speeds in m.p.h. I.A.S:
    Engine assisted   95 to 100
    Glide   110 to 115.

(iv) When lowering the undercarriage hold the lever fully
     forward for about two seconds. This will take the
     weight off the locking pins and allow them to turn
     freely when the lever is pulled back. The lever
     should then be pulled back smartly to the down
     position and left there. It should NOT be pushed
     into the gate by hand. As soon as the undercarriage
     is locked down the lever should automatically spring
     into the gate and the hydraulic valve indicator
     return to IDLE. If it cannot be pulled fully back,
     hold it forward again for at least two seconds. If
     it becomes jammed it may generally be released by a
     smart blow of the hand. If this fails it is
     necessary to take the weight of the wheels off the
     locking pins, either by pushing the nose down
     sharply or by inverting the aeroplane. The lever
     can then be pulled straight back.

(v) If the green indicator light does not come on, hold
     the lever fully back for a few seconds. If this
     fails, raise the undercarriage and repeat the lower-
     ing. If this fails also, use the emergency system
     (see Sect.2, Para.22.).

     Note: Before the emergency system can be used the
            control lever must be in the down position.
            It may be necessary to push the nose down
            or invert the aeroplane in order to get the
            lever down.

(vi) If the undercarriage is lowered too late on the
     approach, with insufficient engine speed to develop
     full hydraulic pressure, the selector lever may
     not automatically spring from the fully back position
     into the gate, so indicating that the operation is
     not complete. This may cause the undercarriage to
     collapse on landing.
     (As previously mentioned, the lever must NOT be
     pushed into the gate by hand). It is advisable,
     therefore, to lower the undercarriage early on the
     circuit prior to landing and not in the later stages
     of the approach.

(vii) The aeroplane is nose-heavy on the ground; the
      brakes, therefore, must be used carefully on
      landing.

20.   MISLANDING

  (i) Raise the undercarriage immediately.

(ii) Climb at about 130 m.p.h. I.A.S. with flaps fully
down.

(iii) Raise flaps at a safe height of about 200 - 300
feet.

21.   AFTER LANDING

(i) Raise the flaps before taxying.

(ii) Change to S ratio once and back to M ratio.

(iii) To stop the engine idle for 2 minutes at 800 - 900
r.p.m., then pull the slow running cut-out and
hold it out until the engine stops.

(iv) Turn OFF the fuel cock and switch OFF the ignition.

(v) Oil dilution.- See A.P.2095/4.

The correct dilution period for this aeroplane is:

Atmospheric temperatures above -10°C: 1 minute.
Atmospheric temperatures below -10°C: 2 minutes.

22.   UNDERCARRIAGE EMERGENCY OPERATION

In the event of failure of the hydraulic system
ensure that the undercarriage selector lever is in
the DOWN position (this is essential) and push the
emergency lowering lever forward and downward.   The
angular travel of the emergency lever is about
100° for puncturing the seal of the cylinder and
then releasing the piercing plunger; it must be
pushed through this movement and allowed to swing
downwards.   NO attempt should be made to return it
to its original position until the cylinder is being
replaced.

January 1943

AIR MINISTRY

Amendment List No.4/A
to
AIR PUBLICATION 1565J
Volume I and
Pilot's Notes.

SPITFIRE F/IX AIRCRAFT

MERLIN 61 ENGINE

Note: Amendment Lists to this Air Publication which
affect the Pilot's Notes are allotted a letter
as well as a number. The letters will run consecutively, omitting I and O. The Pilot's Notes
will be complete if this amendment list has been
incorporated.

---

(1)   SECTION 2   Para.7(ii) Delete "two"
                                    and substitute "three"
                                    and add "and one on the
                                    starboard wing-tip".

(2)   SECTION 2   Remove existing sheet
                                    bearing Paras.9 to 14
                                    and substitute new
                                    sheet supplied herewith.

(3)   SECTION 2   Insert this sheet at end
                                    of Section as authority
                                    for the above amendment.

R.T.P./1686 3675 12/42

A.P.1565 L—P.N.

PILOT'S NOTES

FOR

SPITFIRE 16

PREPARED BY DIRECTION OF THE MINISTER OF SUPPLY

A. Rowlands.

PROMULGATED BY ORDER OF THE AIR COUNCIL

J. H. Barnes.

AMENDMENTS

Amendment lists will be issued as necessary and will be gummed for affixing to the inside back cover of these notes.

Each amendment list will, where applicable, be accompanied by gummed slips for sticking in the appropriate places in the text.

Incorporation of an amendment list must be certified by inserting date of incorporation and initials below.

A.L. NO.	INITIALS	DATE	A.L. NO.	INITIALS	DATE
1	*(signature)*	9/12/54	7		
2	*(signature)*	9/12/54	8		
3			9		
4			10		
5			11		
6			12		

NOTES TO USERS

THESE Notes are complementary to A.P. 2095 Pilot's Notes General and assume a thorough knowledge of its contents. All pilots should be in possession of a copy of A.P. 2095 (See A.M.O.A.718/48).

Additional copies may be obtained by the station publications officer by application on Form 294A in duplicate, to Command Head-quarters for onward transmission to A.P.F.S. (see A.P. 113). The number of the publication must be quoted in full—A.P. 1565L—P.N.

Comments and suggestions should be forwarded through the usual channels to the Air Ministry (T.F.2).

Air Ministry
August, 1949

A.P. 1565L—P.N.
Pilot's Notes
(4ᵗʰ Edition)

SPITFIRE 16

LIST OF CONTENTS

3

OTHER CONTROLS

PART II—HANDLING

PART III—LIMITATIONS

PART IV—EMERGENCIES

PART V—ILLUSTRATIONS   *Fig.*

5

SPITFIRE 16

PILOT'S CHECK LIST

(Excluding Checks of Operational Equipment)

ITEM	CHECK	ITEM	CHECK
1. Weight and balance.	Within permissible limits.	12. Centre plane.	Condition of under surface. Panels secure.
2. Authorisation book.	Sign.	13. Engine.	Condition of propeller and spinner. Cowlings secure. Condition of air intake. Absence of oil and coolant leaks.
3. Form 700.	Sign.		
External checks.			
N.B.—Start at the cockpit entrance on the port side and work clockwise around the aircraft.		14. External fire-extinguisher.	In position.
4. Port mainplane.	Condition of upper surface. Panels secure.	15. Starboard radiator.	Condition. Condition of radiator flap. Absence of coolant leaks.
5. Port flap.	Condition and position. Wing indicator.		
6. Port aileron.	Condition. External control lock removed.	16. Starboard undercarriage.	Condition of fairing. Extension of oleo leg. Brake lead secure. Tyre for cuts and creep. Valve free. Chock in position.
7. Port navigation light.	Condition.		
8. Pressure head.	Cover removed.		
9. Port mainplane.	Condition of under surface and leading edge. Panels secure.	17. Starboard mainplane.	Condition of under surface and leading edge. Panels secure. External aerial secure.
10. Port undercarriage.	Condition of fairing. Extension of oleo leg. Brake lead secure. Tyre for cuts and creep. Valve free. Chock in position.	18. Starboard navigation light.	Condition.
		19. Starboard aileron.	Condition. External control lock removed.
11. Port radiator.	Condition. Condition of radiator flap. Absence of oil and coolant leaks.	20. Starboard flap.	Condition and position. Wing indicator.

ITEM	CHECK
21. Starboard mainplane.	Condition of upper surface. Panels secure.
22. Starboard fuselage.	Condition. Panels secure. First-aid outfit fitted. Panel shut. External aerial secure. Condition of under surface. Condition of identification light.
23. Fin.	Condition. Condition of leading edge.
24. Starboard tailplane.	Condition of upper and lower surfaces. Condition of leading edge.
25. Starboard elevator.	Condition. Trimmer. External control lock removed.
26. Rudder.	Condition. Trimmer. External control lock removed. Condition of tail light.
27. Port elevator.	Condition. Trimmer. External control lock removed.
28. Port tailplane.	Condition of upper and lower surface. Condition of leading edge.
29. Tailwheel.	Tyre for cuts and creep. Valve free.
30. Port fuselage.	Condition. Panels secure.
31. Dispersal area.	All clear around aircraft.

ITEM	CHECK
Internal checks.	
32. Internal control locks.	Removed and stowed.
33. Cockpit canopy.	Security and operation. Canopy open.
34. Undercarriage lever.	Locked down.
35. Pilot's seat.	Adjust for height.
36. Rudder pedals.	Adjust for length.
37. Flying controls.	Gun firing button safe. Full and correct movement.
Cockpit check.	
N.B.—Work from left to right.	
38. Cockpit door.	On latch.
39. Crowbar.	In position.
40. Generator warning light.	On.
41. Rudder trimmer.	Full and correct movement.
42. Elevator trimmer.	Full and correct movement.
43. Pressure-head heater.	Off.
44. Camera master switch.	Off.
45. Booster pump switch.	Off.
46. Carburettor air intake.	Filter in.
47. Rear fuselage tank cock.	Wired off.

ITEM	CHECK		ITEM	CHECK
48. Fuel cut-off control.	Cut-off.		66. Fuel pressure warning light.	On.
49. Throttle.	½ inch open. Adjust friction.		67. Fuel pressurising cock.	Off.
50. Undercarriage indicator switch.	On.		68. Drop tank cock.	Off. Jettison lever down.
51. R.p.m. control.	Maximum r.p.m. position.		69. Windscreen de-icer.	Operation.
52. Ignition switches.	Off.		70. Undercarriage emergency lever.	Vertical position.
53. Pneumatic pressure.	Supply. Delivery to each wheel brake.		71. Downward identification light.	As required.
54. Undercarriage indicator.	Green light on. Night flying blind operation.		72. Pilot's harness.	Adjust and test lock.
55. Oxygen.	Delivery.		73. Brakes.	On.
56. Navigation lights.	As required.		**Start and warm up the engine** (see para. 36).	
57. Flap selector.	Up.		74. Generator warning light.	Out.
58. Altimeter.	Set.		75. Fuel pressure warning light.	Out.
59. Direction indicator.	Caged.		76. Pneumatic pressure.	Supply increasing.
60. Cockpit lighting.	As required.		77. Flaps.	Lower and raise.
61. Magnetic compass.	Serviceability.		78. Direction indicator.	Set with magnetic compass. Uncage.
62. Main fuel cock.	On.		79. Radio.	Test V.H.F. and other radio aids. Check altimeter setting with control.
63. Supercharger gear switch.	Auto. Red light out.			
64. Boost gauge.	Static reading.		80. Radiator flaps.	Depress test pushbutton. Flaps open. Release pushbutton.
65. Fuel gauges.	Contents.			

ITEM	CHECK		ITEM	CHECK
	Run up and test the engine (see para. 37).	94.	Fuel.	Main tank on. Main tank booster pump on.
81. Chocks.	Clear.			
82. Taxying.	As soon as possible test brakes. Direction indicator for accuracy. Artificial horizon for accuracy. Check temperatures and pressures. Check brake pressures. Pressure-head heater on if required.	95.	Carburettor air intake.	Filter in.
		96.	Supercharger.	Red light out.
		97.	Undercarriage.	Down and locked.
		98.	R.p.m. control.	2,850 r.p.m. position.
		99.	Flaps.	Down.
			After landing.	
		100.	Pneumatic pressure.	Supply sufficient for taxying.
		101.	Flaps.	Up.
Checks for take-off.		102.	R.p.m. control.	Max. r.p.m. position.
83. Trim— Elevator Rudder.	Neutral. Neutral.	103.	Booster pump.	Off.
84. R.p.m. control.	Maximum r.p.m. position.	104.	Pressure-head heater.	As required.
85. Fuel.	Contents. Main tank on. Drop tank cock off. Rear fuselage tank cock off. Main tank booster pump on.		**On reaching dispersal.** Stop the engine in accordance with para. 52.	
		105.	Main fuel cock.	Off.
		106.	Ignition switches.	Off.
		107.	Electrical services.	All off.
86. Flaps.	Up.	108.	Undercarriage indicator switch.	Off.
87. Supercharger.	As required. Red light out.			
88. Carburettor air intake.	Filter in.	109.	Direction indicator.	Caged.
89. Harness.	Locked.	110.	Chocks.	In position.
90. Engine.	Clear.	111.	Brakes.	Off.
91. Throttle friction.	Tight.	112.	Internal control locks.	On.
Checks in flight as necessary.				
Checks before landing.		113.	Pressure head.	Cover on.
92. Harness.	Locked.	114.	Form 700.	Sign if necessary.
93. Brakes.	Off. Check pressures.	115.	Authorisation book.	Sign.

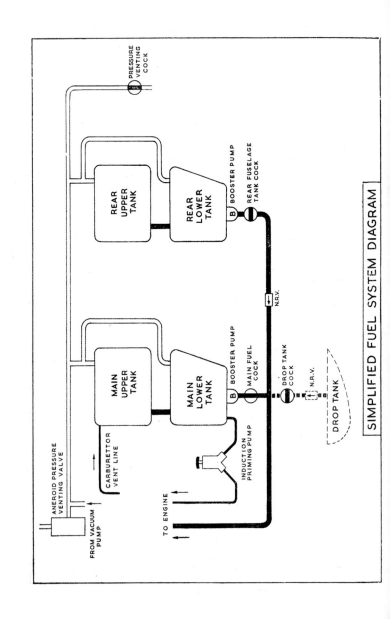

SIMPLIFIED FUEL SYSTEM DIAGRAM

PART I

DESCRIPTIVE

NOTE.—Throughout this publication the following conventions apply :—

    (a) Words in capital letters indicate the actual markings on the controls concerned.

    (b) The numbers quoted in brackets after items in the text refer to the illustrations in Part V.

    (c) Unless otherwise stated all speeds quoted are indicated airspeeds.

INTRODUCTION

1. The Spitfire 16 aircraft is a clipped wing fighter powered by a Merlin 266 engine driving a four-bladed Rotol, constant-speed propeller. An injection type carburettor is fitted. Two 20 m.m. and two .5 inch guns are mounted and there is provision for the carriage of a variety of external stores. Later aircraft have rear-view fuselages with tear-drop canopies.

FUEL, OIL AND COOLANT SYSTEMS

2. Fuel tanks.

  (i) Fuel is carried in two tanks mounted one above the other (the lower one is self-sealing) forward of the cockpit. The top tank feeds into the bottom tank and fuel is delivered to the carburettor, through a filter, by an engine-driven pump. A de-aerator in the carburettor, for separating accumulated air from the fuel, is vented to the top tank. Two additional fuel tanks with a combined capacity of 75 gallons (66 gallons in aircraft with " rear view " fuselages) are fitted in the fuselage behind the cockpit, but their use is prohibited. All the fuselage tanks are pressurised but as booster pumps are fitted pressurising need only be used should the booster pumps fail.

(ii) The effective tank capacities are :—

Top main tank	...	...	...	48	gallons
Bottom main tank		...	...	37 or 47*	gallons

Total main tanks ...   .   85 or 95* gallons

* On some aircraft, generally those with "rear view" fuselages.

(iii) An auxiliary "blister" drop tank can be fitted under the fuselage ; this tank feeds the engine direct and does not replenish the main tanks.

3. **Fuel cocks**

The cock control for the main tanks is a lever (34) fitted below the engine starting pushbuttons and the cock (17) for the rear fuselage tanks is to the left of the pilot's seat. The cock control (38) and jettison lever for the auxiliary drop tank are mounted together on the starboard side of the cockpit, below the undercarriage control unit. The jettison lever is pulled up to jettison the drop tank, but cannot be operated until the cock control is moved forward to the OFF position. The pressurising control (49) is on the starboard side below the windscreen de-icing selector cock (51).

4. **Booster pumps**

A booster pump is fitted in each lower tank ; they are controlled by a three position switch (18) fitted below the elevator trimmer control on the port side. A test pushbutton and ammeter socket are fitted low down on the port side. The booster pumps should not be left switched on when the engine is not running.

5. **Fuel contents gauges and pressure warning light**

The contents gauges (31) on the starboard side of the instrument panel indicate the quantity of fuel in each of the lower tanks when the adjacent pushbutton is depressed.
The fuel pressure warning light (40) is operative when the switch (11) on the throttle quadrant is on and comes on at any time when fuel pressure at the carburettor falls appreciably below normal.

6. **Oil system**

Oil is supplied by a tank of 7.5 gallons oil capacity under the engine mounting ; it is pressurised to $2\frac{1}{2}$ lb./sq. in., and oil passes through a filter before entering the engine. An oil cooler is fitted in the underside of the port wing and oil pressure and temperature gauges are fitted on the instrument panel.

7. **Engine coolant system**

The radiator flaps are fully automatic and are designed to open at a coolant temperature of 115°C. A pushbutton is fitted on the electrical panel for ground testing, and there is a coolant temperature gauge on the instrument panel.

8. **Intercooler system**

The high temperatures resulting from two-stage supercharging necessitate the introduction of an intercooler between the supercharger delivery and the induction manifolds, particularly when S (high) gear is used. An auxiliary pump passes the coolant from a separate header tank to a radiator under the starboard wing, and thence through the supercharger casing to the intercooler, where the charge is cooled by loss of heat passing to the coolant.

MAIN SERVICES

9. **Hydraulic system**

Oil is carried in a reservoir on the fireproof bulkhead and passes through a filter to an engine-driven pump for operation of the undercarriage.

10. **Electrical system**

A 12-volt generator supplies an accumulator which in turn supplies the whole of the electrical installation. A voltmeter across the accumulator is fitted at the top of the instrument panel and a red light, below the test pushbuttons, marked POWER FAILURE, is illuminated when the generator is not delivering current to the accumulator. If the electrical system fails or is damaged, the supercharger will be fixed in or return to low gear and the radiator flaps will remain in or return to the closed position. With a ground battery plugged into the external socket the aircraft accumulator is isolated but all services, including the undercarriage indicator and fuel pressure warning light even if the switch on the engine control quadrant is on, can be tested by means of the ground battery.

11. Pneumatic system

An engine-driven air compressor charges two storage cylinders to a pressure of 300 lb./sq. in. for operation of the flaps, radiator flaps, brakes and guns. If the pneumatic system fails, the position of the radiator flaps will depend on the nature of the failure.

AIRCRAFT CONTROLS

12. Trimming tabs

The elevator trimming tabs are controlled by a hand-wheel (3) on the port side of the cockpit, the indicator (36) being on the instrument panel. The rudder trimming tab is controlled by a small handwheel (2) and is not provided with an indicator. To apply right trim the handwheel is rotated clockwise.

13. Undercarriage control

The undercarriage selector (39) moves in a gated quadrant on the starboard side of the cockpit. To raise the undercarriage, the lever must be moved downwards to disengage it from the slot, inwards through the gate, and then forward to the full extent of the quadrant. The lever should spring outwards through the upper gate and when the undercarriage is locked up it will automatically spring back into the upper slot.

To lower the undercarriage, the lever must be held forward for about two seconds, pulled through the upper gate and then back in one movement to the full extent of the quadrant. The lever should spring outwards through the lower gate and when the undercarriage is locked down it will automatically spring into the lower slot.

When operated in either direction the lever must be permitted to spring outboard when it reaches the end of its travel ; this ensures that it can spring into the appropriate slot when the undercarriage is locked up or down. The lever must not be forced into either slot by hand. An indicator in the quadrant shows DOWN, IDLE, or UP, depending on the position of the hydraulic valve. UP or DOWN should show only during the corresponding operation of the undercarriage, and IDLE when the lever is in either slot. If mishandled or out of adjustment it is nevertheless possible for the lever to be on the wrong side of the gate, and yet for the indicator to show IDLE. It is important to check, therefore, that the lever is correctly positioned in the slot. If, when the engine is not running, the indicator shows DOWN, it should return to IDLE when the engine is started ; if it does not, probable failure of the hydraulic pump is indicated.   For emergency lowering of the undercarriage, see para. 55.

14. Undercarriage indicator

The electrically operated visual indicator (26) has two-semi-transparent windows on which the words UP on a red background and DOWN on a green background are lettered ; the words are illuminated according to the position of the undercarriage. A roller blind is fitted for use at night. The indicator is controlled by the switch (11) on the throttle lever quadrant. On some aircraft, mechanical indicators are fitted for each main wheel. They consist of rods which protrude from the upper surface of each wing when the wheels are down.

15. Flaps control

The split flaps have two positions only, up and fully down. They are controlled by a finger lever on the instrument panel.

16. Wheel brakes

The brake lever is fitted on the control column spade grip and a catch for retaining it in the on position is fitted below the lever pivot. A triple pressure gauge (37), showing the air pressures in the pneumatic system cylinders at each brake, is mounted on the instrument panel.

17. Flying controls locking gear

Two struts are stowed on the starboard side of the cockpit aft of the seat. The longer strut and the arm attached to it lock the control column to the seat and to the starboard datum longeron, and the shorter strut, attached to the other strut by a cable, locks the rudder pedals. The controls should be locked with the seat in its highest position.

ENGINE CONTROLS

18. Throttle

The throttle lever (9) is gated at the climbing boost position. There is a friction adjuster (14) and locking nut (13) on the side of the quadrant. The mixture control is automatic.

19. Propeller control

The r.p.m. control lever is outboard of the throttle lever. Friction is adjusted by the same adjuster as the throttle lever.

20. Supercharger controls

The two-speed, two-stage supercharger automatically changes to high gear at about 11,000 feet on the climb and back to low gear at about 10,000 feet on the descent. An override switch (30) is fitted on the instrument panel by means of which low gear may be selected at any height. There is a pushbutton (22) on the electrical panel for testing the gear change on the ground, and a red light on the instrument panel comes on when high-gear is selected on the ground or in flight.

21. Radiator flap control

The radiator flaps are fully automatic and there is no manual control. A pushbutton for testing the radiator flaps is on the electrical panel.

22. Fuel cut-off

The cut-off lever (7) is fitted outboard of the throttle lever. It is set through the gate to the fully aft position

16

to cut off the fuel. It should be in this position at all times
if a booster pump is switched on when the engine is not
running.

23. **Carburettor air-intake filter control**

On tropicalised aircraft the carburettor air filter control
on the port side of the cockpit has two positions OPEN
and CLOSED (NORMAL INTAKE and FILTER IN
OPERATION on later aircraft). The CLOSED (or
FILTER IN OPERATION) position must be used for
all ground running, take-off and landing and when flying
in sandy or dust-laden conditions.

NOTE.—In the air it may be necessary to reduce speed to
160 knots or less, before the filter control lever
can be operated ; it must always be moved
slowly.

24. **Induction priming pump**

A hand-operated pump (32) for priming the induction
system is fitted below the right-hand side of the instrument panel.

25. **Ignition switches and starter buttons**

The ignition switches (23) are on the starboard side of
the instrument panel and the booster-coil and the engine
starter pushbuttons (33) are forward of the main fuel
cock control. Each pushbutton is covered by a safety
shield.

26. **Ground battery starting**

The socket for starting from an external supply is
mounted on the starboard engine bearer.

O T H E R   C O N T R O L S

27. **Cockpit door**

The cockpit door is fitted with a two position catch which
allows it to be partly opened, thus preventing the canopy
from sliding forward in the event of a crash or forced
landing. It will be found that the catch operates more

easily when the aircraft is airborne than when on the ground.

NOTE.—On aircraft with " tear-drop " canopies, the two-position catch should not be used.

28. Canopy controls

(i) The canopy hood is opened from inside by means of the lanyard fitted at the top forward edge which should first be pulled down to release the catch and then back to slide the canopy open. To prevent the canopy sliding forward unintentionally, care should be taken to ensure that it has been fully opened so that the retaining catch has engaged, and the cockpit door should be partially opened, see para. 60.

(ii) On aircraft with rear view fuselages the "tear-drop" canopy is opened and closed by a crank handle (41) mounted on the starboard cockpit wall, above the undercarriage selector lever. The handle must be pulled inwards before it can be rotated. The canopy may be locked in any intermediate position by releasing the crank handle which then engages with the locking ratchet.

(iii) From outside the cockpit either type of canopy may be opened and closed by hand provided the pushbutton below the starboard canopy rail is held depressed.

29. Guns and Cine-camera

The selective gun firing unit (27) on the spade grip fires the guns and, if selected, the cine-camera. The cine-camera only is fired by means of the pushbutton (35). The camera master switch (19) and footage indicator are on the port side of the cockpit.

30. Bombs and R.P.

The bomb distributor (5) is on the port side of the cockpit. Selected bombs are released or R.P. fired, by means of the pushbutton (10) on the throttle lever.

31. Gun sight

A reflector or gyro gun sight is mounted above the instrument panel. The reflector sight is operated by a dimmer switch marked OFF, NIGHT, and DAY below the mounting bracket. Spare bulbs are stowed in holders on the starboard side of the cockpit. When the gyro gun sight is fitted there is a master ON-OFF switch (42) and a selector-dimmer (43) on the starboard side of the cockpit, and the ranging control is incorporated in the throttle lever.

32. Signal discharger

The recognition device fires one of six cartridges out of the top of the rear fuselage when the handle to the left of the pilot's seat is pulled upwards. On some aircraft a pre-selector control is mounted above the operating handle.

33. Oxygen system

The oxygen master cock (45) is on the starboard side and the regulator (25) is on the port side of the instrument panel. The socket for the mask connection is on the starboard side of the seat.

34. De-icing system

The selector cock (51) and handpump (48) for the windscreen de-icing system are on the starboard side of the fuselage aft of the undercarriage control.

PART II
HANDLING

35. Management of the fuel system

(i) *Use of the booster pump*
The main tanks booster pump should be switched on for take-off and landing and at all times when these tanks are in use in flight.

(ii) *Order of use of tanks*
Main fuel system only

(a) Start the engine, warm up, taxy and take-off on the main tanks.

When a drop tank is fitted

(b) Start, warm up and take-off on the main tanks and change over to the drop tank at a safe height, then turn off the main tanks cock and switch off the booster pump.

(c) When flying at a low altitude, it is recommended that the change over to the main tanks is made before the drop tank is completely empty, working on a time basis. At altitude, it is safe to drain the drop tank completely. When the fuel pressure warning light comes on or the engine cuts, proceed as follows :—

(i) Close the throttle.

(ii) Turn off the drop tank cock, turn on the main tanks cock and switch on the booster pump.

(iii) Idle the engine until it runs smoothly, then open up slowly.

(d) If it is necessary to jettison the drop tank before it is empty, switch on the main tanks booster pump and turn on the main tanks cock before turning the drop tank cock off.

(e) Always ensure that the drop tank cock is in the fully off position after the tank has been emptied or jettisoned ; otherwise, air may be drawn into the main fuel system.

FINAL CHECKS FOR TAKE-OFF

TRIM ... ELEVATOR NEUTRAL

RUDDER NEUTRAL

PROPELLER ... MAXIMUM R.P.M.

FUEL ... CONTENTS

MAIN COCK ON

BOOSTER PUMP ON

FLAPS ... UP

FINAL CHECKS FOR LANDING

FUEL   ... CONTENTS

                MAIN COCK ON

                BOOSTER PUMP ON

BRAKES   ... OFF

                CHECK PRESSURES

WHEELS   ... DOWN AND LOCKED

PROPELLER   ... 2,850 R.P.M.

FLAPS   ... DOWN

36. **Starting and warming up the engine**

(i) After carrying out the external, internal and cockpit
checks detailed in the Pilot's Check List, confirm :—

Main fuel cock	On.
Rear fuselage tanks cock	Wired off.
Drop tank cock	Off.
Fuel cut-off control ...	Fully aft.
Throttle	1 inch open.
R.p.m. control	Maximum r.p.m. position.
Carburettor air intake filter control	Filter in operation.

(ii) If the engine is to be started from an external source
have a ground starter battery plugged in.

(iii) With the fuel cut-off control lever set to off, switch on
the main tank booster pump for 30 seconds to prime the
system. Switch off the booster pump and after a few
seconds, set the fuel cut-off control to on.

(iv) Operate the Ki-gass priming pump until the fuel reaches
the priming nozzles ; this may be judged by a sudden
increase in resistance. High-volatility fuel should be used
for priming at air temperatures below freezing.

(v) Switch on the ignition and prime with the following number of strokes if the engine is cold :—

Air temp. °C.	+ 30	+ 20	+ 10	0	− 10	− 20
Normal fuel	3	4	7	12	–	—
H.V. Fuel	–	–	—	4	8	18

Leave the priming plunger out and press the engine
starter and booster-coil pushbuttons. When the engine
fires release the starter pushbutton but keep the booster-
coil pushbutton depressed until the engine is running
smoothly. It may be necessary to continue priming gently
until the engine picks up on the carburettor.

(vi) Screw down the priming pump, open up gradually to
1,200 r.p.m. and warm up at this speed.

(vii) While warming up, carry out the checks detailed in the
Pilot's Check List, items 74 to 80.

37. **Exercising and testing**

After warming up to 15°C. oil temperature and 40°C.
coolant temperature :—

(i) Test each magneto as a precautionary check before increasing power further.

(ii) Open up to the static boost reading (zero under standard atmosphere conditions) and check the operation of the supercharger by pressing and holding in the test push-button. Boost should rise slightly and the red light should come on when high gear is engaged. Release the test pushbutton, boost should fall slightly and the red light go out on return to low gear.

(iii) At the same boost, exercise and check the operation of the constant speed unit by moving the r.p.m. control through its full governing range at least twice and then return it fully forward. Check that the r.p.m. are within 50 of those normally obtained, and check that the generator warning light is out.

(iv) Test each magneto in turn. The single ignition drop should not exceed 150 r.p.m. If the single ignition drop exceeds this figure but there is no undue vibration, the ignition should be checked at higher power—see below. If there is marked vibration, the engine should be shut down and the cause investigated.

(v) The following full power checks (for which the tail must be securely tied down) may also be carried out after repair, inspection other than daily, when the single ignition drop at the static boost reading exceeds 150 r.p.m., but there is no undue vibration or at the discretion of the pilot. Except in these circumstances, no useful purpose will be served by a full power check.

  (a) Open the throttle fully and check take-off boost and r.p.m.

  (b) Throttle back until the r.p.m. fall, thus ensuring that the propeller is not constant speeding and test each magneto. If the single ignition drop exceeds 150 r.p.m., the aircraft should not be flown.

(vi) After completing the checks either at static boost or full power, steadily move the throttle to the fully closed position and check the minimum idling r.p.m., then open up to 1,200 r.p.m.

38. **Taxying**

(i) Before taxying, carry out the checks detailed in the Pilot's Check List, items 81 and 82.

(ii) While taxying, the brakes should be used with care and, particularly in high winds, sudden bursts of high power should be avoided.

39. Take-off

(i) Carry out the checks detailed in Pilot's Check List, items 83 to 91.

(ii) At normal loads, $+7$ to $+9$ lb./sq. in. boost is sufficient for take-off, but power should be increased to $+12$ lb./sq. in. on becoming airborne. Any tendency to swing to port can easily be checked with the rudder.

(iii) The aircraft should be flown off at a speed of approximately 95 knots.

(iv) After raising the undercarriage, see that the red indicator light—UP—comes on. It may be necessary to hold the lever through the gate and at the top of the upper slot until the red indicator light does come on. Failure of the wheels to lock up will spoil the airflow through the radiators and oil cooler and result in excessive engine temperatures.

(v) As speed increases, directional retrimming will be necessary.

(vi) Set the air intake filter control as required.

40. Climbing

(i) (a) The speed for maximum rate of climb is 140 knots from sea level to 25,000 feet reduced thereafter by 10 knots for every 5,000 feet.

(b) For normal operation, the recommended climbing speed is 155 knots from sea level to operating height.

(ii) *Climbing at maximum rate of climb using climbing power* With the switch set to AUTO, the supercharger will automatically change to high gear at about 11,000 feet. This is the optimum gear change height for a full power climb. Under normal climbing conditions (2,850 r.p.m. $+12$ lb./sq. in. boost), the maximum rate of climb is obtained by delaying the gear change until the boost has dropped to $+8$ lb./sq. in. To do this proceed as follows :—

Set the supercharger switch to M.S., the r.p.m. control lever to give 2,850 r.p.m. and climb at the speed given in (i) (a) opening the throttle progressively to maintain a boost pressure of + 12 lb./sq. in. When the maximum obtainable boost drops to + 8 lb./sq. in. set the supercharger switch to AUTO throttling back to prevent overboosting as the change to high gear is made.

(iii) *Climbing using maximum power*

Set the supercharger switch to AUTO and open the throttle fully.

(iv) *Climbing for maximum range*

Set the supercharger switch to M.S., the r.p.m. control lever to give 2,650 r.p.m. and climb at the recommended range speed (150 knots) opening the throttle progressively to maintain + 7 lb./sq. in. boost. Set the supercharger switch to AUTO when the maximum obtainable boost is + 3 lb./sq. in., throttling back to prevent over boosting as the change to high gear is made.

(v) Use of the air intake filter considerably reduces full throttle height.

A.L. 2
Para. 41
(i) (ii)

41. **General flying**

(i) *Stability*

At all loads stability about all axes is satisfactory, but the application of excessive yaw promotes a marked change of longitudinal and lateral trim.

(ii) *Flying in turbulent conditions*

The recommended speed up to 25,000 ft. is 175 knots.

42. **Controls**

(i) The controls are light and well harmonised and the aircraft is easy and pleasant to fly. The elevator and rudder trimming tabs are powerful and sensitive and should be used with care.

(ii) *Changes of trim*

Flaps down	...	...	...	Nose up
Flaps up ...	...	...	...	Nose down

Movement of the undercarriage in either direction or operation of the canopy promotes little change of trim. Changes of power and speed induce marked changes in directional trim. These should be countered by careful and accurate use of the rudder trimming tab. The firing of salvoes of R.P.'s promotes a nose up change of trim which is most marked in level flight at about 260 knots.

(iii) *Flying at reduced airspeed*

Reduce speed to 140 knots and lower the flaps. Set the r.p.m. control lever as required and open the canopy. Fly at about 120 knots. The stalling speed under these conditions is 55 knots.

43. Cruising for maximum range

The speed for maximum range at normal loads is 150 knots. At heavy loads, it is recommended that this speed be increased to 170 knots. This will not incur any serious loss of range.

44. Fuel consumptions

The approximate fuel consumptions (gals./hr.) are as follows : —

(i) *Weak mixture* (as obtained at +7 lb./sq. in. boost and below) :

Boost lb./sq. in.	R.P.M.				
	2650	2400	2200	2000	1800
+7	80	—	—	—	—
+4	71	66	61	54	—
+2	66	61	57	50	43
0	60	55	51	45	39
−2	53	49	45	40	35
−4	45	42	38	34	30

(ii) *Rich Mixture* (as obtained above +7 lb./sq. in. boost) :

Boost lb./sq. in.	R.p.m.	gals./hr.
+15	3,000	130
+12	2,850	105

NOTE.—Accurate figures giving the variation in consumption with height and as between low and high gear are not available.

45. Position error correction

From ...	105	130	145	180	210	250	Knots
To ...	130	145	180	210	250	300	I.A.S.
Add ...	4	2	0	—	—	—	Knots
Subtract ...	—	—	0	2	4	6	

46. **Stalling**

(i) The approximate stalling speeds in knots are :—
With full main tanks and full ammunition :—

Power off—Undercarriage and flaps up ...	70–75
„ „ —Undercarriage and flaps down ...	60
Power on—Under typical landing conditions	50–55

With external stores these speeds are increased by 5 to 10 knots.

(ii) There is very little warning of the approach of the stall, especially with power on, but slight buffeting may occur some 5-10 knots before the stall. At the stall either wing and the nose drop together. Continued backward pressure on the control column results in pronounced tail buffeting and an increased tendency for either wing to drop. Stalling speeds and characteristics remain unaffected with the canopy open.

(iii) If the aircraft is stalled in a turn, or in the recovery from a dive, slight warning is given by tail buffeting. At the stall the aircraft may flick in either direction.

(iv) Recovery in all cases is straightforward and easy.

47. **Spinning**

(i) Practice spinning is permitted and recovery by the standard method is normal.

(ii) During the spin the nose rises and falls slightly but the rate of rotation remains substantially constant.

(iii) Recovery action should be initiated after not more than two turns of the spin have been completed and a speed of 140-160 knots should be attained before easing out of the resultant dive.

(iv) Practice spinning should not be commenced below 10,000 feet.

(v) Spinning is not permitted when external stores are carried.

48. **Diving**

As speed is gained, the aircraft becomes increasingly tail heavy and should, therefore, be trimmed into the dive although it can be held to the limiting speed without retrimming. The tendency to yaw to the right should be trimmed out by accurate use of the rudder trimming tab. The rudder trimming tab becomes very sensitive at high speed.

49. Aerobatics

(i) The following speeds in knots are recommended :—

Roll	...	...	...	200–220
Loop	...	...	...	260–280
Half roll off loop	...	...	...	280–300
Upward roll	...	...	...	300 plus

(ii) Flick manœuvres are not permitted.

(iii) Aerobatics are not permitted when carrying any external stores (except the 30 gallon blister type drop tank).

50. Approach and landing

(i) Carry out the checks in the Pilot's Check List, items 92 to 99.

(ii) The recommended speeds in knots at which the airfield boundary should be crossed are :—

	At maximum landing weight Flaps down
Engine assisted...	90
Glide	100

(iii) The initial approach should be made some 20 knots above these figures.

(iv) The brakes should be used with care on landing.

51. Mislanding and going round again

(i) The aircraft will climb away easily with the undercarriage and flaps lowered, and the use of full take-off power is unnecessary.

(ii) Open the throttle steadily to the required boost.

(iii) Raise the undercarriage.

(iv) Climb at about 120 knots with the flaps lowered.

(v) Raise the flaps at a safe height and retrim.

52. After landing

(i) Before taxying, carry out the checks detailed in the Pilot's Check List, items 100 to 104.

(ii) (a) After reaching dispersal, if the serviceability of the engine is in doubt, such items of the run-up given in para. 37 as may be necessary should be carried out. In all cases, however, the engine should be idled at 800-900 r.p.m. for a short period and if no other check of the ignition has been made, the magnetos should be tested for a dead cut. To stop the engine the throttle should be fully closed and the fuel cut-off control moved to the off position.

(b) The correct oil dilution period for this engine is :—
1 minute at atmospheric temperatures *above* – 10°C.
2 minutes at atmospheric temperatures *below* – 10°C.

(iii) When the engine has stopped, carry out the checks detailed in the Pilot's Check List, items 105 to 115.

PART III
LIMITATIONS

53. Engine limitations : Merlin 266

The principal engine limitations are :—

	S/c gear	R.p.m.	Boost	Temp. °C. Coolant	Oil
MAX. TAKE-OFF 5 MINS. LIMIT	Low	3,000	+18	135	—
MAX. CLIMBING 1 HOUR LIMIT	Low } High }	2,850	+12	125	90
MAXIMUM CONTINUOUS	Low } High }	2,650	+ 7	105(115)	90
COMBAT 5 MINS. LIMIT	Low } High }	3,000	+18	135	105

The figure in brackets is permissible for short periods.

OIL PRESSURE :
    MINIMUM IN FLIGHT   ...   30 lb./sq. in.

MINIMUM TEMP. °C. FOR TAKE-OFF
    COOLANT   ...   .   *40°*C.
    OIL   ...   .   +15°C.

54. Flying limitations

(i) *Maximum speeds in knots*

Diving (without external stores), corresponding to a Mach. No. of .85 :

Between S.L. and 20,000 ft.	385
„ 20,000 and 25,000 ft. ...	370
„ 25,000 and 30,000 ft. ...	335
„ 30,000 and 35,000 ft. ...	290
Above 35,000 ft.	265
Undercarriage down	140
Flaps down	140

Diving (with the following external stores) :

(a) With 1 × 500 lb. 58 bomb, or 1 × 65 bomb
    Below 20,000 ft.*   380

(b) With 1 × 500 lb. S.A.P. bomb or smoke bomb
    Below 25,000 ft.*   345

    (c) With 10 lb. practice bomb
                Below 25,000 ft.*   360

    * Above these heights the limitations for the "clean" aircraft apply.

(ii) *Maximum weights in lb.*

    For take-off and gentle manœuvres only   ...   8,700*
    For take-off and all forms of flying and landing 7,450
    * At this weight take-off must be made only from a smooth hard runway.

(iii) *Flying restrictions*

    (a) Rear fuselage tanks should never be used or filled.

    (b) Aerobatics and violent manœuvres are not permitted when carrying any external stores (except the 30-gallon " blister " type drop tank).

    (c) When wing bombs are carried in addition to a drop tank or fuselage bomb, take-off must be made only from a smooth hard runway.

    (d) When carried, the 90-gallon drop tank must be jettisoned before any dive bombing is commenced.

    (e) Except in emergency the fuselage bomb or drop tank must be jettisoned before landing with wing bombs fitted.

    (f) Drop tanks should not be jettisoned unless necessary operationally. While jettisoning, the aircraft should be flown straight and level at a speed not greater than 260 knots.

PART IV
EMERGENCIES

55. **Undercarriage emergency operation**

(i) If the lever jams and cannot be moved to the fully down position after moving it out of the gate, return the lever to the fully forward position for a few seconds to take the weight of the wheels off the locking pins, thus allowing the latter to turn freely, then move it to the DOWN position.

(ii) If, however, the lever is jammed so that it cannot be moved either forward or downward, it can usually be released by taking the weight of the wheels off the locking pins either by pushing the control column forward sharply or inverting the aircraft. The lever can then be moved to the DOWN position.

(iii) If the lever springs into the slot and the indicator shows that the undercarriage is not locked down, hold the lever at the bottom of the slot for a few seconds. If this is not successful, raise and then lower the undercarriage again.

(iv) If the undercarriage still does not lock down, ensure that the lever is in the DOWN position (this is essential) and push the emergency lever (46) forward and downward through 110°. On some aircraft the label quotes 90° : this is incorrect. The CO_2 cylinders will then lower the main wheels. The lever should not be returned to its original position and no attempt must be made to raise the undercarriage until the emergency bottles have been replaced.

Note.—If the CO_2 cylinders have been accidentally discharged with the selector lever in the up position, the undercarriage will not lower unless the pipeline from the cylinder is broken, either by hand or by means of the crowbar.

56. **Failure of pneumatic system**

(i) If the flaps fail to lower when the control is moved to the DOWN position, it is probably due to a leak in the pipeline resulting in complete loss of air pressure and the brakes will also be inoperative.

(ii) Alternatively, if a leak develops in the flap control system the flaps may lower, but complete loss of air pressure will follow and the brakes will become inoperative. In this case a hissing sound may be heard in the cockpit after selecting flaps DOWN.

(iii) In either case, the flap control should immediately be returned to the UP position in order to allow sufficient pressure to build up, so that a landing can be made with the brakes working, but without flaps.

(iv) As a safeguard, pilots should always check the pneumatic supply pressure after selecting flaps DOWN. If the pressure is low and does not build up a landing without brakes must be anticipated, although sufficient air may remain for their partial use.

57. **Flapless landing**

Make the initial approach, with or without power at about 115 knots aiming to cross the airfield boundary at 100 knots. The aircraft requires a long landing run.

58. **Canopy jettisoning**

(i) The canopy may be jettisoned in an emergency by pulling

the rubber knob inside the top of the hood forward and downward and then pushing the lower edge of the canopy outwards with the elbows.

(ii) Before jettisoning the canopy the seat should be lowered and the head then kept well down.

59. **Jettisoning of external stores**

(i) The drop tank, and in emergency the fuselage bomb, can be jettisoned manually by pulling up the jettison handle mounted outboard of the seat on the starboard side.

(ii) Drop tanks should not be jettisoned unless operationally necessary. During jettisoning the aircraft should be flown straight and level at a speed not in excess of 260 knots.

(iii) Underwing stores can be jettisoned manually by pulling the handle (16) mounted below the instrument panel on the port side.

60. **Crash landing**

In the event of engine failure necessitating a crash landing :—

(i) If oil pressure is still available the glide can be lengthened considerably by setting the r.p.m. control fully back past the stop on the quadrant.

(ii) The external stores or drop tank should be jettisoned.

(iii) The fuel cut-off control should be pulled fully back and the booster pump switched off.

(iv) The canopy should be opened and the door set on the catch.

(v) A speed of at least 130 knots should be maintained while manœuvring with the undercarriage and flaps retracted.

(vi) The harness should be tight and locked.

(vii) Flaps should not be lowered until it is abundantly clear that the selected landing area is within easy gliding reach.

(viii) The final straight approach should be made at a speed of 85-90 knots with the undercarriage retracted.

61. **Ditching**

(i) Whenever possible the aircraft should be abandoned by parachute rather than ditched, since the ditching qualities are known to be poor.

(ii) When ditching is inevitable any external stores should be jettisoned (release will be more certain if the aircraft is gliding straight) and the following procedure observed :—

(a) The canopy should be jettisoned.

(b) The flaps should be lowered in order to reduce the touchdown speed as much as possible.

(c) The undercarriage should be kept retracted.

(d) The safety harness should be kept tightly adjusted and locked and the R/T plug should be disconnected.

(e) The engine, if available, should be used to help make the touchdown at as low a forward speed as possible.

(f) Ditching should be along the swell, or into wind if the swell is not steep, but the pilot should be prepared for a tendency for the aircraft to dive when contact with the water is made.

62. **Crowbar**

A crowbar (4) for use in emergency is stowed in spring
clips on the cockpit door.

63. **First-aid outfit**

A first-aid outfit is stowed on the starboard side in the
rear fuselage. It is reached through a hinged panel.

PART V
ILLUSTRATIONS

AIR MINISTRY
September, 1949

Amendment List No. 1
to A.P. 1565L—P.N.

SPITFIRE 16

The incorporation of this Amendment List must be certified by inserting date of incorporation and initials in the spaces provided on the inside of the front cover.

	AMENDMENT
Cover	*Insert* " 4th Edition '' in top left-hand corner.
Page 3	*Insert* " 4th Edition '' beneath the A.P. number in top right-hand corner.

Affix this Amendment List to inside back cover of the Notes.

AIR MINISTRY
September, 1951

Amendment List No. 2
to A.P. 1565L—P.N.
Pilot's Notes

SPITFIRE 16

The incorporation of this Amendment List must be certified by inserting date of incorporation and initials in the spaces provided on the inside front cover of the Pilot's Notes.

PART	PAGE OR PARA.	AMENDMENT
List of contents	Page 4	*Delete* "Signal discharger . . . . . 32".
I	Para. 32	*Delete* this paragraph.
II	Para. 41	*Amend* by gummed slip herewith.
III	Para. 53	*Alter* minimum coolant temperature for take-off to 40°C.

Affix this Amendment List to inside back cover of Notes retaining A.L.1.